∞

The Inner Life
of Jesus

Other books
by Romano Guardini
available from Sophia Institute Press:

Eternal Life
The Art of Praying
The Rosary of Our Lady
And the Word Dwelt Among Us
Learning the Virtues That Lead You to God
Preparing Yourself for Mass
Living the Drama of Faith
The Lord's Prayer
The Living God

The Inner Life of Jesus
Pattern of All Holiness

by
Romano Guardini

SOPHIA INSTITUTE PRESS®
Manchester, New Hampshire

The Inner Life of Jesus: Pattern of All Holiness was originally published in Germany in 1957 by Werkbund-Verlag, Würzburg, under the title Jesus Christus: Geistliches Wort. In 1959, Henry Regnery Company published an English translation by Peter White entitled Jesus Christus: Meditations. This 1998 edition by Sophia Institute Press uses the 1959 Henry Regnery translation, with minor editorial revisions throughout the text.

Sophia Institute Press®
Box 5284, Manchester, NH 03108
1-800-888-9344

Nihil obstat: J. Gerald Kealy, D.D., Censor theol. deput.
Imprimatur: Albert Gregory Meyer, S.T.D., S.S.L.
Archbishop of Chicago, June 15, 1959

Library of Congress Cataloging-in-Publication Data

Guardini, Romano, 1885-1968.
[Jesus Christus, geistliches Wort. English]
The inner life of Jesus : pattern of all holiness / Romano Guardini.
    p.   cm.
ISBN 0-918477-84-0 (pbk. : alk. paper)
1. Jesus Christ — Sermons. 2. Catholic Church — Sermons.
3. Sermons, German — Translations into English. I. Title.
BT202.G7613   1998
232 — dc21   98-30731   CIP

99 00 01 02 10 9 8 7 6 5 4 3 2

Contents

Editor's Note: except where otherwise noted, the biblical quotations in the following pages are from Msgr. Ronald Knox's translation of the New Testament. Where applicable quotations have been cross-referenced with the differing numeration in the Revised Standard Version, using the following symbol: (RSV =).

∞

The Inner Life
of Jesus

Chapter One

The Key to Approaching
the Mystery of Jesus

Blessed art thou
who hast believed.
Luke 1:45

∞

To attain a full understanding of a tree as it is, we must look into the earth, where its roots are, from which the sap rises into the trunk, twig, blossoms, and fruit. Similarly, we shall do well to consider now that earth from which the personage of our Lord arises: Mary, His mother.

We are told that she came of noble parentage, royal blood. Now, every man is unique, created but once, with an identity belonging to him alone. And in that which is peculiarly his own, in what he is when he stands face-to-face with himself and God, the particular circumstances which produced him are of no account. There is no why or wherefore here; "there is neither Jew nor Greek; there is neither bond nor free."[1] Quite true.

Yet in matters of great moment, and ultimately even in all the affairs of life, everything depends on whether a person is of noble quality or not. So it is here. In the simple generosity of Mary's answer to the Angel of the Annunciation, a most noble quality came to light, royal in character.

Something tremendous confronted her. What was being asked of her was nothing less than blind surrender into the hands of God. Precisely this surrender is what she gave, with a

[1] Gal. 3:28.

quiet greatness, wholly unselfconscious. A good part of this greatness of soul sprang from her nobleness of being, her sheer uncluttered stature.

And from this time forth, her destiny was linked to her Child's: first by the bitterness that came between her and her betrothed; then by the journey to Bethlehem, where she bore her Child in surroundings of poverty and want; then the flight and exile to a foreign country — her way of life upset, full of danger, taken with such suddenness from the security she had always known — until it was safe to go home again.

When her Child was twelve years old and stayed behind in the temple and she found Him again only after an anxious search, then for the first time the divine mystery was revealed in which her life was caught up. Her seemingly well-founded reproach, "Son, why hast Thou done so to us? Behold Thy father and I have sought Thee sorrowing!" was answered in a tone of astonishment (and the tone must have been the most unnerving thing of all): "How is it that you sought me? Did you not know that I must be about my Father's business?"[2]

Then indeed Mary must have had some inkling of what the future held for her. There must have been a foreknowledge that Simeon's prophecy would be fulfilled: "And thy own soul a sword shall pierce."[3] For how could one interpret such a thing as a child answering his frightened mother in this situation by asking, with fullest confidence in the self-evident rightness of his position, "How is it that you sought me?" It is

---

[2] Luke 2:48-49.
[3] Luke 2:35.

not surprising to read what follows: "And they understood not the word that He spoke unto them."[4]

However, we read directly after, "His mother kept these words in her heart."[5] She could not understand the word that He spoke; she was not equal to the situation in the way of intellectual comprehension, but she was indeed equal to it in the way of being a person of enough gravity to take it in, like the good soil that takes into itself a rare and precious seed which then begins to grow there.

Then follow eighteen years of tranquillity. The holy Gospel tells us nothing further about them. But when the ear is properly tuned for it, this silence of the Gospels speaks with a great voice. Eighteen years of silence going by "in her heart": we are told no more than that the Child "was subject to them" and "advanced in wisdom and age and grace with God and men"[6] — tranquil, profound surroundings, ever in the presence of the love of this holiest of all mothers.

Then He went forth from His home and into His mission, His destiny. But she was still with Him. At the beginning, she was at the marriage-feast of Cana, where a last remnant of maternal protectiveness and correction can still be seen. Another time, when some sort of disturbing news must have found its way to Nazareth, she bestirred herself to look Him up, and stood there waiting at the door.[7] Again she was with Him in His last days, and stood under the Cross.

[4] Luke 2:50.
[5] Luke 2:51.
[6] Luke 2:51-52.
[7] Mark 3:31-32.

The Inner Life of Jesus

The entire life of Jesus is surrounded by the deep significance of having His mother close by. The strongest message of all comes out of her silence.

One word may give us some indication of how profound the affinity was between the Lord and His mother. He is standing in the midst of the people, teaching them, when suddenly a woman's voice speaks out: "Blessed is the womb that bore Thee, the breast which Thou hast sucked!" And Jesus answers, "Shall we not say, 'Blessed are those who hear the word God and keep it'?"[8] It is as if all at once He has drawn away from the noise and hubbub of the crowd, as though a bell has sounded deep in this soul . . . and He is in Nazareth with His mother.

Elsewhere, however, if we listen to the words which Jesus speaks to His mother and simply let them make their impression upon us just as they arise out of the situation, it is as if a gulf opens up between Him and her every time.

That time in Jerusalem — when He was still a child and, without a word to her, had stayed behind, when all the city was in a state of unrest and He could have been injured, not simply by accident, but by foul play — surely then she had the right to ask Him why He had acted as He did. But He answers her with astonishment: "How is it that you sought me?" And as we wait for a further word of explanation, some bridging of the gulf, we read only this: "And they understood not the word that He spoke unto them."

He attends the wedding-feast at Cana in Galilee. The family are obviously people of modest means, who have little in the way of worldly possessions. The wine gives out, and everyone

[8] Luke 11:27-28.

senses the mounting embarrassment. Mary comes to Him, beseeching, "They have no wine left." How does He reply? "Nay, woman, why dost thou trouble me with that? My time has not come yet."[9] What does that mean other than this: "My concern is to do the will of my Father, as He shows it to me moment by moment — that is my time. With that you have nothing to do." To be sure, a little later, He does help her. But that is because His time *has* come, not because she beseeched Him.

She comes down from Galilee seeking Him, perhaps again "sorrowing"; but He is busy inside a house teaching. They tell Him, "Behold Thy mother and brethren are without, looking for Thee." He asks, "Who is a mother, who are brethren, to me?" And He looks at the people sitting in a circle around Him and says, "Here are my mother and my brethren! If anyone does the will of God, he is my brother and sister and mother."[10] And, although He surely did go out and greet His mother lovingly, yet the words that He had spoken still lay between them.

Right here, feeling the shattering effect of His rebuke, spoken with such sternness, we become aware of the infinite distance out of which He comes, and the depth of the gulf which lies between Him and her. Yes, the very incident which shows their closeness to each other also shows the distance between them. "Blessed is the womb that bore Thee, the breast which Thou hast sucked." No! "Shall we not say, 'Blessed are those who hear the word of God and keep it'?"

[9] John 2:3-4.
[10] Mark 3:32-35.

And the last time, when He was on the Cross, with the end near, while His mother stood below, yet nonetheless bound to Him in all the torment of her heart, hanging, waiting on a word from Him, He said to her, with John in mind, "Woman, behold thy son," and to the beloved disciple, "Behold thy mother."[11] Surely, it must have been troubling. But in her heart, she must have sensed the meaning of that other sentence: "Woman, behold thy son." He was telling her to be quit of Him. He was now wholly engaged in that "hour" which had come, great and terrible and demanding everything. In the ultimate, solitary presence of God, with the sins of the world laid upon Him, before God's justice, there He was indeed quite alone.

Mary stood ever by His side. All that befell Him she shared. Indeed His life was her life. But not in the sense of intellectual understanding: "The Holy Spirit" — how full of meaning is that word *the* in the message of the Angel of the Annunciation,[12] how pregnant with the mystery and remoteness of God! — the Holy Spirit came upon her "from on high," that which is great beyond measure. She gave the Holy Spirit all she had: her heart, her honor, her blood, and all her power of love. She enclosed the Holy Spirit, and the Holy Spirit grew out and over her. A remoteness came upon her Son; the Holy Spirit, in whom He lived, apart from her.

In the end, she could not understand Him. How could she understand the mystery of the living God? But she did what in a Christian sense is almost equal to understanding, which can

[11] John 19:26-27.
[12] Luke 1:35.

be done only by that same divine power which makes understanding possible: she believed. If anything shows her grandeur, it is the words of her cousin Elizabeth: "Blessed art thou who hast believed!"[13] It accounts for her more than the other two phrases: "And they understood not the word that He spoke unto them," and again, "Mary kept all these words in her heart."[14]

Mary believed. It was demanded of her that she constantly renew this faith, that it might become ever firmer, more bare of supports — greater. She had faith greater than anyone has ever had. Abraham underwent a terrible test of his faith,[15] but more was demanded of her than of Abraham. For the Holy One sprang from her, grew away from her, went on past her — the Holy One, who drew His being from a different order, apart from her.

Yet she did not make a natural womanly underestimation of His greatness due to having borne Him, and nourished Him, and seen Him in His helplessness. She did not give in to a mother's usual temptation to demand of her son that she always remain mother, the one who holds him in her arms, so that when he is grown and she can no longer hold him, she wants him to be smaller, to make him a child once again.

Nor was she to mistake her love for Him when He went forth from the simplicity of her protection. Above all she believed this was as it should be; the will of God was thus being fulfilled. She never slackened, never quit the scene, never

---

[13] Luke 1:45.

[14] Luke 2:50, 51 (Douay-Rheims edition).

[15] Gen. 22:2 (Douay-Rheims edition).

grew small-minded, but chose rather to persevere, to follow, through the power of faith, every step her Son took in all its unfathomableness. That was the measureless quality of her greatness.

Every step the Lord took toward His divine destiny Mary took with Him — not in the way of understanding, but in the way of faith. Only at Pentecost did real understanding come to her. Then she understood all those things which up to that time she, believing, had "kept in her heart."

Let us open ourselves up to this. Here she is closer to Christ, more profoundly engaged in the work of Redemption than she is in all the miracles told in legendary stories. These can delight us with their enchanting pictures, but we cannot live by them — least of all when we are being tried in adversity. What is asked of us is that we wrestle in faith with God and with whatever opposes us in the world. It is not the faith of cheerful fables that is demanded of us in these times, but rather a hard faith, for the softening and accommodating enchantment is falling away from all things, and everywhere the contradictions collide roughly with one another.

The more thoroughly we allow ourselves to mingle with the figure of the Mother of God in the New Testament, the more substance there is to our real Christian life. She was the one who encompassed the Lord with all her being through His whole life, and in death as well. She was the one who had to experience Him, who came from God, growing ever further away from her. Time and again He raised Himself above her, and time and again, feeling the edge of the sword, she increased her faith to match His new stature, and encompassed Him anew — until at the end, He was no longer her Son. The other one, who stood beside her, was to be her son now. But Jesus remained alone up there, on the sharpest pinnacle of Creation, in the presence of God. She received this separation in a final act of sharing His suffering, and once again, in this very act, she stood by Him in faith.

Yes, verily, blessed art thou who hast believed.

Chapter Two

The True Figure of Christ on Earth

As long as I am in
the world . . .
John 9:5

∞

A man's life is a weft of happenings of every sort. People and things are there, friendly and hostile, close or alien. They work their influence; they hinder or further. Man comes to grips with the realities of the world; he has dealings; he acts, creates, and experiences his destiny. This plethora of elements is all drawn together by what we call his personality. Here is something very important: what is the total impression this man makes?

There are different ways of looking at this.

One man's career appears to us like the lifespan of a tree, at first visibly growing out of the ground, then gently unfolding itself, gradually reaching its full growth, and dying. In such a person, there is a hardy contemporaneousness drawn from the outside world: he finds himself at home there.

Another gives us the impression that he is looking for his mission in life, finds and occupies his post, works, struggles, and after he has done his duty, he drops away.

And again there is the restless type, ever seeking, ever in transit, incapable of living any other way but through danger and discovery.

There is the man of destiny, in close touch with whatever moves in the very womb of being; such a one waits, makes his encounter, grows to great stature or shatters, perseveres, and bears his burden.

The Inner Life of Jesus

The ultimate figure cut by the life of our Lord does not belong in any of these categories. If we read the Gospels in a connected way and look for the reverberations of His person in the Acts of the Apostles and the apostolic letters, and then ask ourselves, "Just what was He like?" we sense something quite special: something that eludes classification. Perhaps we may best express it with the words "He passed by." The shape and form of Jesus' being is a passage.

This fact is expressed right off by how very little we know about Him. St. John says at the end of his Gospel that if all that Jesus had said and done were to be written, the world itself could not contain the books that would thus be filled.[16] Thus the apostle must have been aware of an awesome abundance of being within Jesus. Behind every moment, every word, every act of this being, there stood infinite intensity, measureless content.

But what has been passed on concerning Him is not very much. If we draw together the accounts in the Synoptic Gospels — those of the first three evangelists, who give a simultaneously witnessed report of Christ — with whatever else is said that is new, if we take the very special things St. John says and the little that can be found in the Acts of the Apostles: all this put together is really not very much! Of the first years of His life we learn of a few youthful episodes. Then eighteen years are wrapped in silence. His effectiveness in public is presented under a very bright light; but it lasts only three years — some say very little more than one year. Then it is all over. This life comes out of the silent unknown, shines

---

[16] John 21:25.

briefly and mightily, then returns to the unknown reaches of Heaven.

Jesus Himself speaks of this coming and going. "It is for this that I have come," He says when it is a question of His not staying where He is, but going rather "to the next country towns."[17] In Matthew, three times in a row He says, "I have come to . . .";[18] this phrase occurs frequently in other passages.

In the Gospel according to St. John, this awareness comes out very strongly, more so than anywhere else. Time after time: "I have come"; and, "After a little while, you will see me no longer";[19] "I am going away to prepare a home for you";[20] "Whither I go you cannot come."[21]

This feeling that He comes, passes by, and then disappears is even stronger on those occasions when He mentions where He is from and where He is going: "From on high";[22] "from the Father"; again "back to the Father"; where the "everlasting dwellings"[23] are. "It was from the Father that I came, when I entered the world, and now I am leaving the world, and going on my way to the Father."[24]

That particular interior character shows also in the manner of His life. He lived as an itinerant teacher, which in those

---

[17] Mark 1:38.
[18] Cf. Matt. 10:34-35.
[19] John 16:16.
[20] John 14:2.
[21] John 13:33.
[22] Cf. John 8:23.
[23] Luke 16:9.
[24] John 16:28.

times was not at all uncommon. Without any real home, He went from place to place, instructed, held conversation with the people there, and stayed wherever anyone would have Him. He was deeply, intensely aware that this was His state in life. When the young man asked if he might follow Him, He answered, "Foxes have holes, and the birds of the air their resting places; the Son of Man has nowhere to lay His head."[25]

He must often have been well received. We are put in mind chiefly of that house He loved, the house of Lazarus and his sisters, in Bethany.[26]

But sometimes it did not go so well with Him, as on the occasion when Simon the Pharisee invited Him. Immediately we sense ambush. He was not hospitably received; He was "surrounded." When the woman came up to Him and wept at His feet, dried them with her hair, and anointed them with precious ointment, the master of the house displayed contemptuous scorn: "If He were a true prophet, He would know what sort of woman this was!" Then Jesus turned to the host: "Simon, there is something I have to say to thee. I came into thy house; thou gavest me no water for my feet; thou embraced me not; thou gavest me no oil upon my head for anointing."[27] He meant, "You did not fulfill the most elementary obligations of hospitality for me." We would say that the company simply did not receive Him. And it is most affecting to read how this courtesy was bestowed on Him by someone rejected by this same company.

[25] Luke 9:58.
[26] Cf. John 12:1-2.
[27] Luke 7:36-40, 44.

But did He not have a home with His own, in the understanding of His disciples, in the fidelity of those who were His followers?

One fact stands out very clearly in the Gospels, a painful one, all the more true for having been recognized by the Apostles themselves in the light of their subsequent inspired insights: the disciples did not understand Him. Often St. Luke writes, "But they could not understand what He said; it was hidden from them so that they could not perceive the meaning of it."[28]

Again and again this is plainly indicated, now in words, now in manner, now in deed. St. John says, "In Him there was life, and that life was the light of men. And the light shines in darkness, which was not able to master it."[29] The light wanted to come streaming out of Him, to make men's hearts and minds clear, but, like a great wall, the darkness stood round about Him, the darkness of nonunderstanding. He was full of life, ready at all times to pour it into men's hearts, but they were shut against it.

And what about love, fidelity? One betrayed Him; another denied under oath ever having known Him; and in the end, the rest all fled — even John. Even John abandoned Him at first, but then he returned and stood his ground. No, the feeling of home given by a protective understanding, where word and deed find their proper sanctuary, and fidelity which endures unshaken: these comforts were not for Him. There, too, "the Son of Man had nowhere to lay His head."

[28] Luke 9:45.
[29] John 1:4-5.

It is an expression of this always being on the outside of things when we read again and again that He went forth to pray, by Himself alone, in the quiet of the night, on a high mountain. At such time, He is in that same sphere out of which He emerged to begin His public mission. Then hardly had He been baptized in the Jordan when St. Mark tells us, "And immediately the Spirit drove Him into the desert."[30] The Spirit "drove Him," as if by force, away from the community of mankind, out, into the desert. And in order that we know without any mistake what that represents, the Gospel says further, "And He was in the desert forty days and forty nights . . . and He was with beasts."[31] And there in the solitude, out of touch with everything that had to do with men, the Tempter sought Him out.

Most affecting is that scene after the Last Supper, when He was going out of the city with His disciples, and crossing over the brook Kidron, on His way up to the Mount of Olives. There He left the group behind Him, taking along only the three; once again He asked them to wait, going on alone "a stone's throw off."[32]

This was the figure our Lord cut during His earthly life, the character of His "passage."

When we come up close to someone, we look at him. And we not only look over his exterior, to see what he looks like, what his name or identity might be, where he comes from, from what walk of life, but we probe also with an interior

[30] Mark 1:12 (Douay-Rheims edition).
[31] Mark 1:13.
[32] Luke 22:41.

glance: "Who are you?" Not only, "What manner of man are you?" — to know what to expect of him; but the more searching "Who are you?" — to know him truly, to come close to him in an interior way, to meet him face-to-face, eye-to-eye.

In the same way, we are to ask the Lord, "Who art Thou?" We do not know very much if we know only the words and the episodes handed down to us concerning Him. We do not know very much if we carry a picture of Him in our mind as a ceremonial, somewhat unreal, indefinite figure with long hair and a robe with many folds. All that is only a phantom, a delusion. His whole being must ring in our hearts with blood and bone. We must follow Him. We must strive to penetrate into the heart of His mystery, to what He really is. Then things become plain to us, as we have found them here.

Chapter Three
∞

How Jesus Transforms
Failure into Success

Unless the grain of wheat falls
into the ground and dies . . .
John 12:24

We have looked into what sort of a presence Jesus was, at the character of His earthly existence. We thought to find the answer in considering Him as one who "passed by." He was in the world, entered into the life of the world, into everything that makes it the kind of world it is. He took upon Himself the human condition, in its profoundest depths as well as its externals. He held back in nothing. He truly became "one of us, like us in all things except sin."[33]

But the manner in which He was all these things, the characteristic of His existence in the world of men, was that of someone passing by.

And when we go deeply into ourselves, we can feel that sublime unknown that was in Him. Put this same question once again, thus: "What did all His dealings and His struggles and His doings add up to?" And the answer is, they all took the shape of failure.

Is it not almost a precondition for failure that He who set out to be the Savior of the world should have been born in Palestine, no more than a tiny corner of the world of that time? No one of importance could really take it seriously. When Christ's accusers try to advise as to the proper procedure in the

---

[33] Heb. 4:15.

matter, we mark the lack of esteem in Pilate's answer: "Am I a Jew?"[34]

And again, the place where He was born was that very bit of this small corner of the world which the Jewish people itself had the least regard for: Galilee. When Philip came to Nathaniel saying, "We have discovered who it was that Moses wrote of in his law, and the prophets, too; it is Jesus the Son of Joseph, from Nazareth," we read astonishment in the answer: "Can anything that is good come from Nazareth"[35] — anything worth taking seriously?

This signifies a choice already made for a particular mode of being: whether it should begin in the center of things, or off in a corner somewhere; where life is most vigorous and intense, or otherwise.

Even with such a background as this, if success was what He wanted, the obvious step would have been to get out of Galilee into the part of the country that was the marketplace of intellect and ideas, where history was made. Or still more likely, leave Palestine behind and go out into the great world. This would have been quite easy to do. When He said to the Jews, "You cannot reach the place where I am," they must have thought to themselves, "Could He be going into the Greek Diaspora to teach the Greeks?"[36] But Jesus never left His native land. Only once did He pass through heathen territory, near Tyre and Sidon.[37] That must have made a deep

---

[34] John 18:35.

[35] John 1:45-46.

[36] Cf. John 7:34-35.

[37] Matt. 15:21.

impression on Him. He must have sensed something of the great world outside Palestine and the much freer, more open humanity there. A hint of this comes in the words of doom: "Woe to thee, Chorazin; woe to thee, Bethsaida! Tyre and Sidon would have repented long ago, humbling themselves with sackcloth and ashes, if the miracles done in you had been done there instead."[38] The Lord must have recognized the same thing often so oppressively manifest to us: the broader, finer, more straightforward human qualities are often found elsewhere than in the household of the Faith. But His mission called for remaining "with the sons of the House of Israel."[39]

In fact, He never set out for Jerusalem to see the wise men of the country, the scribes, the educated people. And these are not here mentioned in scorn. It is an unfortunate habit, not uncommon among religious people, to look down on the great works of the world, creations of the mind, values of the productive life, and struggles of various political entities. These things, too, are from God and destined for His greater glory.

There was much seriousness, wisdom, sense of responsibility, and sense of sacrifice among those scribes and Pharisees — thrown in with all the narrow-mindedness, hardness of heart, and untruthfulness that Jesus exposed in them. They preserved the inheritance of the past. They carried the responsibility for the spiritual inheritance of the people of Israel. From a purely human point of view, it would have been quite worthwhile to go see them. Jesus did not do so. In John's Gospel, we catch some of this attitude of His when His brethren,

---

[38] Luke 10:13.
[39] Cf. Matt. 15:24.

scornful and unbelieving, say to Him, "This is no place for Thee; go to Judea, so that Thy disciples also may see Thy doings. Nobody is content to act in secret, if he wishes to make himself known at large; if Thou must act thus, shew Thyself before the world!"[40]

Jesus did not show Himself "before the world." All His life He was among small townsfolk, "little people." And in truth, it represents a denial of great proportions to give up frequenting the great and the powerful and to remain in the world of little people. There is a lot of narrowness, pettiness, self-righteousness, and haughtiness in that kind of a world! How many great-hearted, soaring ideas, how many mighty thoughts have been stifled by that atmosphere! But Jesus was not exactly one of these little people. He was descended from kings.

Is it not a frightful limitation that He lived for such a short time? We take it for granted that He lived until His thirtieth year hidden away in obscurity, was publicly active very briefly thereafter, and died in the fullness of His manhood. But let us seek to understand what might have been.

Suppose Jesus "advanced in wisdom and age and grace with God and men"[41] — not just up to His thirtieth year, but thereafter as well. Suppose that one age after another were manifested in Him; all the successive stages of human existence unfolded in Him, all possibilities of speaking, acting, and struggling, until in the end, we were to see Him as a man of eighty, or a hundred. How wonderful that would have been! Jesus as full of years as Abraham; Jesus as old as Moses. What a

---

[40] John 7:3-4.

[41] Luke 2:52 (Douay-Rheims edition).

fullness of wisdom, what a mighty power of love, what capacity to act, what majesty would there be personified!

Instead of all that, just two short years. All those tremendous possibilities ruined. This marvelous being constantly thwarted, closed in. And finally, when His active career had hardly begun, He was destroyed.

Well, then, let His life be for only a short time! But at least a short time of radiant glory, great thundering victories!

But in fact — let us come out with it — He failed in everything. Hardly had He begun to spread His message, scarcely had the divine powers within Him begun to manifest themselves and He had started drawing people to Him, when the opposition began forming. Mistrust awaited Him in ambush. His enemies banded together, and it was on the side of authority and responsibility that they formed ranks.

What would have been a success? Perhaps if He had joined battle with His enemies, who were after all people of some consequence, and by the power of His Spirit, the divine light that shone from His countenance, the purity of His love — in short, by being the Person He was — He had persuaded them and made them recognize: Truly this man is "He who is to come."[42]

Once every so often He did convince someone. There was the teacher of the law who, upon hearing Jesus' answer to his question as to which was the first and greatest commandment, answered, "Master, Thou hast spoken truly"; and Jesus could say to him, "Thou art not far from the kingdom of Heaven."[43]

[42] Matt. 11:3; Luke 7:19.
[43] Mark 12:32, 34.

There were those who were together with John and believed; and there were others, too.

But all should have been won to be over — that would have been victory. But Jesus did not win such a victory. They did not allow themselves to be convinced. They were obsessed with the idea that He was a seducer, and thought so the more as they sensed the greater power working within Him.

It would have been success if at least by the power of His personality, He had brought them to silence; if they had had to withdraw and show that He was right. But that did not happen either. They were silent enough when His answer stung them; but right away, they would again try to bait Him. Finally, they got the upper hand, brought Him up for a trial, and sentenced Him to an execution not only terrible, but also degrading, so He might appear totally discredited as a Savior before His people, whose Savior He wished to be.

He addressed Himself to ordinary people. What opportunity for victory lay there? If He had won the people's hearts by His infinite love, His divine undeviating certitude, until they had been ready to say, "Truly with such a man there is salvation," that would have been a victory. But this did not happen. He detected the motives of those who came streaming toward Him: "Because you have been given bread to eat, therefore you come."[44] To some extent, they were drawn by a yearning for salvation, by some feeling of being in a divine presence, but their approach was vacillating, curious, and earthly. And when, after the initial successes, the enemies went to work, it was plain that the people were no more than a mob, without

[44] John 6:26.

any sense of direction. It would have been a success if He had managed to get the people to come to His rescue. If only some of them had stuck by Him. But in the end, they all clamored their preference for Barabbas, the robber-hero.[45]

Did He not even triumph in the hearts of His followers? Victory in this instance would have meant conquering them interiorly: making them understand Him from the depths, making them devoted to Him in love and unwavering fidelity. But we know the way it went: He was the Light, but the darkness pitted itself against Him like a solid wall, and He did not overcome it, as we understand *overcome* in a human sense, breaking through with a historic act, so the light shines and success shows.

Now let us look even deeper. Let us examine the struggle going on in the plane of the invisible, beneath the events of history, against the forces of the Demon.

The Enemy approached Him first in the desert. The Lord put him to flight. Then we are told, "So the Devil, when he had finished tempting Him in every way, left Him in peace until the time should come."[46] But he returned. He returned in the form of those diabolical forces playing upon the sick who gave lip-service to the honor of Christ and at the same time tried to spread confusion in the surroundings. He returned in the ever-growing hatred of His enemies, who eventually came to feel that any means of opposing Him was justified. He returned in the soul of the traitor. And in the end, we are told, "Your time has come now, and darkness has its will."[47]

---

[45] Luke 23:18.

[46] Luke 4:13.

[47] Cf. Luke 22:53.

In the sense that He might have achieved a clear victory over the powers of darkness, He did not win out. In the historical sense, they defeated Him. But at the same time, He knew well that, in God's order, "I have mastered the world."[48]

The abiding figure of Jesus' life is failure, defeat. Humanly speaking, there has never been a great personality, filled with the glories of the Spirit and endowed with grace, who came to such a wretched end as He did. Unless we open ourselves to this fact, the figure of our Lord and His earthly life may appear trivial and idyllic, and its immense majesty will escape us.

Jesus knew this. Words like these show how well He knew it: "He who loves his life will lose it; he who is an enemy to his own life in this world will keep it so as to live eternally"; "a grain of wheat must fall into the ground and die, or it remains nothing more than a grain of wheat; but if it dies, then it yields rich fruit."[49] Jesus speaks in these passages for whoever has ears to hear the whole secret of Christian living, which is the way of suffering, and reaches its divine fulfillment only through earthly failure and defeat. But He speaks out of the mystery of His own being: "Was it not to be expected that the Christ should undergo these sufferings, and enter into His glory?"[50]

Failure lies at the heart of the life of Christ. It points the way, like the notion of passage, to the understanding of His intimate self.

[48] John 16:33.
[49] John 12:25, 24.
[50] Luke 24:26.

Chapter Four
∞

Christ's Power to Draw Us Close to Him

For He taught them like
one who had authority.
Matthew 7:29

∾

We have examined the figure of Christ and His mode of being. We have done what one tries to do when looking at a painting, finding the perspective, the elements of the composition, the message the artist tried to convey, and we came upon two meaningful characteristics. In the first place, He was one passing through, as He Himself once said: "It was from the Father that I came, when I entered the world, and now I am leaving the world and going on my way to the Father."[51] And we found that He performed His mission through failure: the grain of wheat had to die.[52]

This catches our attention. We feel there must be something extraordinary about such a person.

But now, put that aside, as it is not our purpose here to construct a connected discourse on the being of Christ. With love, reverence, open eyes, and sentient hearts, we are trying to penetrate to the image of His figure in life; to look at a number of times over, first from one viewpoint, then from another, in order to examine each trait separately, and to bring them together in a synthesis in the hope that we will find the essential reality, like a gift that has been given to us.

[51] John 16:28.
[52] Cf. John 12:24.

So now let us ask what effect He had upon the people, how they responded to Him, and what sort of commotion was created around Him.

People must have felt there was something very special about this man. Their attention was aroused. They were held fast. They were agitated, upset, deeply stirred. They valued Him and did Him honor. They also felt irritated, became mistrustful, hostile, and grew to hate Him.

All this has great meaning — most of all because none of the positions people took concerning Him originated in the intelligence alone, but all derived from a direct motion of the heart. There was something particular about Him which gripped people, radiating from Him, a force that made itself felt all around Him. This meant that all who saw Him were involved in a special way, passionately aroused to love or hate — to very special love, or very special hate.

Let us try to find out more about this.

Right at the beginning of His mission, after the Sermon on the Mount, we read, "Afterward, when Jesus had finished these sayings, the multitudes found themselves amazed at His teaching. For He taught them, not like their scribes and Pharisees, but like one who had authority."[53]

Now, the scribes were well-instructed people. They reflected a lot, and worked hard. Their sayings were learned and to the point. But their words were cold and hard, rigid, oppressive. And now here stood one whose words were warm, full of power. Jesus' power derived from what He said, from the depth and the truth of the spoken word — but not from that alone.

[53] Matt. 7:28-29.

More than anything else, it came from the vitality sounding through His speech, from the vital energy of Him who spoke. Everything about Him was genuine, strong, and straight from the mind and heart. It was candid, rang true, had radiance, and contained an effective principle of life. It sent out a call; it wakened, lifted up, cleared the mind, and clutched at the heart. And there was warranty behind it, an assurance of salvation.

Once at Passover time in Jerusalem, He went into the temple. It was a time of pilgrimage. Believers came from all over the world to pay homage to God in His glory. The same sort of fair that always springs up around pilgrimages was going on here too: sellers' booths; dealers in every kind of merchandise; sacrificial animals, so that anyone could buy one and offer it and thus fulfill his obligation as a pilgrim. Moneychangers were on hand who accepted foreign coins in exchange for the currency of the country. Haggling and greed and the smell of money were everywhere the order of the day.

All of this filled Jesus with anger, and there followed a scene such as there had been in the days of Elijah and Elisha, when the Spirit of God came over the prophets and, with the suddenness of divine inspiration like a flash of lightning, did wondrous things beyond ordinary human understanding. "It is written," He cried, 'My house shall be known for a house of prayer,' and you have made it into a den of thieves."[54] He made a whip by binding cords together and drove everything and everyone out, people and animals. There is a note of gentleness in the midst of this divine whirlwind, when He spared the

---

[54] Matt. 21:13.

doves, saying only, "Take these away!"[55] He overturned the tables of the moneychangers; everything was in an uproar. But in all the heat of that moment, among the mob there, collected from all the corners of the earth, no voice was raised against Him, not one hand. As St. Jerome[56] writes, "Something like a star shone from His countenance," transfixing them all.

There was another occasion in Nazareth, in the synagogue. He asked for the book and read aloud this passage from Isaiah: "The Spirit of the Lord is upon me; he has anointed me and sent me out to preach the gospel to the poor, to restore the broken-hearted; to bid the prisoners to go free and the blind to have sight; to set the oppressed at liberty, to proclaim a year when men may find acceptance with the Lord, a day of retribution."[57] He rolled up the scroll text and gave it back to the temple servant. The eyes of all present fastened on Him, and He then said, "The scripture which I have read in your hearing is today fulfilled."[58]

He made known the message of this fulfillment. They heard; they felt the overmastering power, but they shut themselves against it. He noticed the resistance. He laid bare before them what they were thinking: "If Thou art the Promised One, prove Thyself. Perform the miracles the Promised One is to do! Right now, here before us. If Thou art the 'physician,' why dost Thou not 'heal Thyself' — that is to say, us, the people of

[55] John 2:16.

[56] St. Jerome (c. 342-420), Biblical scholar.

[57] Isa. 61:1-2; Luke 4:18-19.

[58] Luke 4:21.

Thine own country?"[59] But instead He spoke to them of the mystery of how those standing closest by could be unseeing and cast out, while those a distance away could understand and be made whole.

Then their wrath was kindled against Him. They drove Him out of the city, led Him to the top, the "brow," of the hill on which their city was built, to the place where it drops down abruptly, in order to cast Him over the precipice to the bottom. And then — we know today how a mob like that behaves in such a situation — comes the incredible sentence: "But He passed through the midst of them and went on His way."[60]

Not a word, not a gesture. An unspoken self-confidence in almighty power.

He taught by the seaside, and said to Peter, whom He had shortly before made one of His followers, "Stand out into the deep water, and let down your nets for a catch." Peter knew the sea. The time to fish was at night. "Master, we have toiled all the night, and caught nothing, but at Thy word, I will let down the net." And they cast out the nets, and their boats nearly sank with the weight of the catch. Peter was overcome, and he threw himself down on his knees: "Leave me to myself, Lord. I am a sinner!"[61]

We must not interpret this as some sort of tame humility. It is quite another thing. The fear of God came over him. The same thing that happened so often in the history of Israel, the awful reality of God overwhelming someone and the fright of

[59] Cf. Luke 4:23.

[60] Luke 4:30.

[61] Luke 5:4-8.

it casting him to the ground — this is what happened here: The quivering, sinful creature shrieks out, "Go! Go away!"

The true spirit of a man shows itself in the sort of people who feel drawn to Him.

The children must have loved coming to Him; otherwise their mothers would never have brought them. Nor would He have wanted to see them, all fatigued as He must have been in the late afternoon. Anyone whom children like to be with understands how to get along with them and knows what to say to them; anyone good with children and animals — for He loved animals, too; it showed in the metaphors He used — is a person with a breath of Paradise hovering over him.

The sick came streaming to Him. It reveals a great deal about a man if the suffering press themselves upon Him because they feel they are welcome to do so. It is generally otherwise; the painfully ill most often feel that they are being shunned. Has it not always been so that the sick are cared for according to the best principles of science and charitable administration in order that suffering may be abolished? But how about the one who suffers: does he feel warmly received in this process? It would seem there is less and less room in the world for suffering. A modern city does everything possible so that misery of any kind will no longer be encountered within its gates. Suffering is ever more and more discreetly eliminated. There is something extraordinary, beautiful, and frightening about a man upon whom the suffering press themselves. Such a thing will devour him. The relief of suffering is paid for with the stuff of blood and heart. They kept coming to Jesus, from every corner. From the side streets and hovels, from all sides, this dark, embittered army pressed upon Him. He laid His hands upon them, raised them up, touched them, cleansed them, and made them whole.

There is an account of an episode that can affect one deeply. It happened in the district of the Gerasenes. A man possessed was in a fit, naked and distraught, terrifying everyone, and tormenting himself. The man caught sight of Jesus from afar; drawn as by force, he stumbled along toward Him, and while he was still some distance off, a voice cried out from him, "Why dost Thou meddle with me, Jesus, Son of the most High God? I pray Thee, do not torment me!" But Jesus subdued the powers of darkness, quieted the man down, and by the time people had gathered around to see, the unfortunate fellow was sitting at Jesus' feet, decently dressed, peaceable, and talking perfectly sensibly from a mind that had been cured. Jesus tried to send him away, but he wanted to stay. He felt protected where he was; nothing sinister had any power near this Man, so he resisted until Jesus to him, "Return to thy home, and recount all that God hath done for thee."[62]

Such incidents abound.

Around Jesus there was life stirring. Something worked within Him: in the words He spoke, giving them life, power over mind and heart; in the commands from His lips, through the gestures of His hand; and no could resist. It radiated from His frame and His head, and made people draw back. It came driving out of His being, unnerving people. It drew to Him everyone with an open and a clean heart, so that when they were together with Him, they felt they had come home. This power within Him spoke out some message wherever there

---

[62] Luke 8:26-39.

was suffering and tribulation, making people come to Him and find relief. It brought peace and drove away the powers of darkness.

What words can we find for it? It must have been the very thing that is meant by His message from the kingdom of Heaven: the holy immanence of the living God. It means that God is here present, filling a heart to its deepest recesses, overwhelming a will completely, the one and the all of a living soul. It means that here is a being for whom God represents total blessedness, a being completely permeable by Him; so that He can speak through Him, address anyone who approaches — that is what is meant by the immanence of the holy, living God.

And more yet than mere immanence — but there will be another occasion to dwell on that.

Chapter Five

How Christ Relieves
Our Sufferings

And they brought unto
Him all the sick.
Matthew 4:24

∽

Christ heals the sick. On the very first pages of the Gospels, He appears as the healer. He had hardly begun His teaching when the sick started coming. They were brought to Him from every quarter. It was as if the masses of the afflicted were always opening up around and closing in on Him. They came by themselves, they were led, they were carried, and He passed through the suffering multitude of people, and "a power from God was present, and healed."[63]

From the nameless crowds, certain individuals keep coming forward, characterized by the Evangelists in a few strokes of the pen.

Right at the beginning, He came up to Peter's house. Peter's mother-in-law was ill with a bad fever. He approached the litter, and standing over her, He "rebuked the fever." It left her, and straightaway she rose and attended to the visitors.[64]

Christ went on His way, and many followed along. A blind man sitting by the roadside, heard the crowd's agitation, asked who He was, and called out, "Jesus, Son of David, have pity on me!" They tried to make him be quiet, but he would not allow himself to be intimidated; he called out ever louder until Jesus

[63] Luke 5:17.
[64] Matt. 8:14-15.

had the man brought before Him: "What wouldst thou have me do for thee?" "Lord, give me back my sight!" And Jesus said, "Away home with thee; thy faith has brought thee recovery." Right on the spot, he was able to see again, and he followed along the way after Him.[65]

Another time, the Lord was sitting in a house, one of the small one-room houses to be found around Galilee. The place was packed about Him, everyone listening all around. No one could get in through the door, it was so crowded. Outside some people were carrying a man crippled with arthritis. When they were unable to get past the door, they got up on the roof, made an opening, and let down the stretcher. The listeners within murmured. But Jesus saw a great uncomplicated faith and comforted the frightened cripple: "Son, thy sins are forgiven." All about the room indignation fermented: "He is talking blasphemy! Who can forgive sins but God, and God only?" Then Jesus set His seal upon the act: "Rise up, take thy bed with thee, and go home." And the cripple did this.[66]

Once again He found Himself in the midst of an audience of hostile listeners, who were judging Him harshly. A man was brought in with a withered hand. It was the Sabbath, and everyone was watching as if to trap Him, wondering what He would do. He told the sufferer to come forward into the center so all could see his affliction. "Which is right: to do good on the Sabbath day, or to do harm? To save life or to make away with it?" And sensing the stupid brutality of their hardened hearts, He looked about Him angrily, as if He meant to compel

[65] Mark 10:46-52.
[66] Mark 2:1-12.

every one of them to see the truth of the situation. Then He said, "Stretch out thy hand!" And it was restored.[67]

Then from the nameless multitudes came each one forward with his affliction, one after the other, barely described, yet speaking to us like life itself. Each situation illustrated the profound, holy power that radiated from Him.

At times, one is prompted to look behind the outward events at the inner working of this sacred power.

A blind man came to Him. Jesus put His hands on the man's eyes, drew them away, and asked, "What seest thou?" All overcome with excitement, the man answered, "I can see men as if they were trees, but walking!" The healing power reached into the nerves. They were revivified, but they did not yet work properly. So He put His hands on the eyes once again, and the man saw things as they were.[68] Does not this story give one a sense of experiencing the mystery, as it were, from behind the scenes?

Another time, there was a great crowd about Him. A woman afflicted many years with a hemorrhage, who had sought everywhere in vain for a cure and had spent all her money to find one, said to herself, "If I can even touch His cloak, I shall be healed." And she came up to Him from behind, touched His garment, and noticed in her body that the distress which had been plaguing her for so long was at an end. But He turned around: "Who touched my garments?" The Apostles were dumbfounded: "Canst Thou see the multitude pressing so close about Thee, and yet ask, 'Who touched

---

[67] Mark 3:1-5.
[68] Mark 8:23-25.

me?' " But He knew just what He was saying; immediately He had been "inwardly aware of the power that had proceeded from Him." And the woman came up to Him trembling, threw herself at His feet, and confessed what had happened. But He forgave her freely and lovingly.[69]

What an effect that had all around! He seemed charged with healing power, as if He needed no intention. If someone approached Him in an open-hearted, petitioning state of mind, the power simply proceeded from Him to do its work.

What did the act of healing mean to Christ? It has been said that He was the great friend of mankind. Characteristic of our own time is an extremely alert sense of social responsibility and responsiveness to works of mercy. So there has been a corresponding desire to see in Him the towering helper of men, who saw human suffering and, out of His great mercy, hastened to relieve it.

But this is an error. Jesus is not a personification of the big-hearted charitable nature with a great social conscience and an elemental power of helping others, going after human suffering, feeling its pangs in sympathy, understanding it, and conquering it. The social worker and the relief worker are trying to diminish suffering, to dispose of it entirely, if possible. Such a person hopes to have happy, healthy people, well-balanced in body and soul, live on this earth. We have to see this to understand that Jesus had no such thing in mind. It does not run counter to His wishes, but He Himself was not concerned with this. He saw too deeply into suffering. For the meaning of suffering, along with sin and estrangement from

---

[69] Mark 5:25-34; Luke 8:43-48.

God, was to be found at the very roots of being. In the last analysis, suffering for Him represented the open road, the access back to God — at least the instrument which can serve as access. Suffering is a consequence of guilt, it is true, but at the same time, it is the means of purification and return.

We are much closer to the truth if we say Christ took the sufferings of mankind upon Himself. He did not recoil from them, as man always does. He did not overlook suffering. He did not protect Himself from it. He let it come to Him, took it into His heart. As far as suffering went, He accepted people as they were, in their true condition. He cast Himself in the midst of all the distress of mankind, with its guilt, want, and wretchedness.

This is a tremendous thing, a love of the greatest seriousness, no enchantments or illusions — and therefore, a love of overwhelming power because it is a "deed of truth in love,"[70] unbinding, shaking things to their roots.

Once again we must see the difference: He did this, not as one carrying on his shoulders the black tragedy of the human condition, but rather as one who was to comprehend it all, from God's point of view. Therein lies the characteristic distinction.

Christ's healing derives from God. It reveals God, and leads to God.

With Christ, healing always appears in some connection with faith. He could perform no miracles in Nazareth because there no one believed.[71] His disciples were unable to cure the

[70] Cf. Eph. 4:15; 1 John 3:18.
[71] Matt. 13:58; Mark 6:5.

sick boy because their faith was on too small a scale.[72] When the man crippled with arthritis was brought up to Him, at first Jesus seemed not to see the man's affliction at all. He saw his faith, and bestowed forgiveness upon him. The blind man heard Him say, "Thy faith has brought thee recovery."[73] The centurion heard the hearty compliment: "Believe me, I have not found faith like this, even in Israel."[74]

Healing belongs to faith, even as the Annunciation belongs with faith. By healing, Jesus revealed Himself in action. Thus He gives concrete expression to the reality of the living God. To make men penetrate to the reality of the living God — that is why Christ healed.

[72] Matt. 17:19-20.
[73] Mark 10:52.
[74] Matt. 8:10; Luke 7:9.

Chapter Six

Seeing Jesus Anew with the Eyes of Faith

He who sent me is true.

John 8:26

∞

Two veils keep us from seeing the living truth of Jesus. One veil is our ignorance. We must admit to ourselves that we really know very little of Him. We may make an effort about many things, following through with care and energy; but have we ever put the same serious effort into listening, questioning, reading, and researching into the matter of who Jesus is?

We are very ignorant about Him. That is a fact. The other veil is that we think we know, but in truth we are just accustomed to hearing the same words, episodes, and statements over and over again. And this habit excludes any possibility of a fresh impression, beclouds the vision even more thoroughly than knowing nothing. Therefore we have a double purpose throughout these meditations: to seek always a new viewpoint from which to examine, question, and explore; and thus to allow ourselves to cast off the gray mantle of custom so that we might get through to the freshness that is the figure of Christ.

What makes a man a Christian is his faith, that inner life that awakens in him the revelation handed down to us from the very moment he receives it.

So now we shall pose this question: What has Jesus to do with this faith? We do not mean by this, "What does He say about faith?" or, "How does He lead one to this faith?" or,

"What does He demand of the believer?" but rather: *Is He Himself a believer?*

When Jesus speaks of the Father, is He speaking from faith? There is a current notion of Jesus and His relation to God which goes as follows: Jesus was a man like us, in every way one of us. Just as we do, so also did He seek salvation. Just as we have been promised, so He, too, found His salvation in His relationship to God. This is what makes Him so great, the fact that He was a man, even though the most exalted one and the closest to God. For that reason, so it goes, He really has a claim to be our Master and Leader. He belongs in the same category as we, albeit much more advanced. His life has the same direction as ours — from the human toward the divine. Therefore He must have been a believer — a believer with the power of a creator, who found the Christian faith in the form we know it, and at the same time living it for all to see; but He also believed.

There is something magnificent in this conception. Within it there is a special desire to be genuinely serious about Christianity. But this conception holds that such seriousness is possible only if the one who brought this Christian attitude into the world is merely one of us. Therein lies the element of strength, the appeal of the idea, the tie that binds, the anchor in human nature.

A great deal could be said on this. The most important point is that in such a conception, Redemption is left out entirely. This disposes of the profoundest fact in Christianity. But disregarding that, let us open the New Testament and see for ourselves how Jesus stands with God, how He speaks of Him, what position He takes when He speaks of God — and we will have to admit that there is no trace whatever of the foregoing. When we put aside all of our preconceived notions and really let the Gospel speak, we must conclude that Jesus is not a believer.

Just what is meant by *faith?*

Let us imagine someone who has never yet heard anything about the Christian Revelation, or has never really been reached by it. One day he comes upon a book mentioning Christianity, or he gets to know someone well who is a Christian in good standing, and so he acquires a feeling for it. A discussion begins, questions go back and forth; there is an approach, and a backing away; the stranger begins to take up the matter, makes great progress — until one day he faces the final decision and takes the step into faith. In the course of these exchanges, he has come upon a new truth within the realm of man's being. In making this decision, he has permitted this truth to get through to him and brought his most private self to bear upon it. Thus faith means getting into communication with God's reality as it appears in the Revelation handed down to us; it means hanging on to this truth, this reality, and living by it.

And this involves risk and effort, rearrangement and the transformation of one's own being toward this reality, and what stems from it. One will be troubled now and then. Sometimes this reality is vividly, powerfully present; sometimes it is veiled: it withdraws itself. Sometimes what this truth demands of us is quite obvious; other times it is not at all clear. Or this truth might be in the full familiar view of the eye of the spirit when suddenly some new factors enter in, new demands are made; and everything, so certain before, is again open to question.

Back of all that has been said, this reality is something that comes from "on high"; that which is in man originates "from below."[75] There is opposition: man will not surrender; he hesitates to permit the passing away of the "old man" in himself.[76] So faith means a constantly recurring struggle for faith, combat, mastery, and perseverance until the next certitude is won.

Someone born in the Faith will have other experiences, but he, too, will always have to go through a more or less total crisis of faith; and even after he has gotten back on his feet again, his faith will continue to encounter difficulties and must be maintained by a struggle.

It is true that faith will grow, as the believer gets to know more and more; from *pistis* (taking things on faith), *gnosis* (recognition of the truth of things believed) will be more and more forthcoming. Once again he is under tension, and the tension must be overcome anew.

Having arrived at this point, if we now look at Jesus and put the question: "Was He a believer?" the only straightforward answer can be no. He makes no breakthrough from unbelief to faith. With Him there was never a question of the shattering of His first childish attachments to the faith by a succession of crises, whence His faith always emerged strengthened and renewed. In Jesus we find no difficulties of belief, no attacks made on His faith, no struggles and victories of that kind. In fact, we find no trace of an attitude of faith in Him, none of the bearing of a man who is grasping a reality that confronts him and reveals itself to him, and sets in motion a conflict

[75] John 8:23.
[76] 2 Cor. 5:17.

between his former frame of reference and one newly awakened, with all the disturbance and self-mastery that goes with such a thing. Here there is no encounter with something that reveals itself, no accepting of something offered.

We may express it in the following way: What Jesus declares, He owns. He possesses the God of whom He speaks. There is no duality here, only unity.

One does indeed sense a profound, mysterious "struggle." There are tensions and conflicts. These arise from the circumstance that Jesus appears to be taking a human view of things. (We will have more to say on this later; it is another subject, and has nothing to do with faith.) Now, one might say, "Very well, so Jesus was not a believer. He was an illuminated person. He was not the one for whom the Word of God was intended, to whom it was delivered by a messenger of faith, in order that He might receive it into His belief. He was the one who brought the Word of God; He was the messenger, the one who had been sent. He had known all these things through interior revelation."

Then we must examine the personalities who we know for certain received the Word by revelation, the ones who had been sent — namely, the prophets. Where do they stand?

In the life of a prophet, there always comes the moment when God lays His hand upon him. Before, he was a believer among all the other believers. Then the hand of God touches him, and thenceforth he is God's instrument. His entire life as a prophet plays itself out in tension between his human, earthly being and this touch from God. What he must perform is not faith, but it is indeed more difficult than faith. The struggle is more difficult, the crises are more profound and more shattering, and the ever-recurring obstacles are harder to overcome. We have only to look at the life of Elijah in the book of Kings or read Isaiah carefully to sense this.

And if, after doing this, we return to Christ and pose the question: "In the strict sense of the word, was He a prophet?" once again our answer is no.

We do not find any divine seizure, first illumination, or disclosure of mission. Some have thought to find this in the Baptism in the Jordan, but it does not stand up. The Baptism in the Jordan discloses a mission,[77] true enough, but it does not initiate one. And we do not find in His life that conflict between the human and the prophetical personalities. Those sacred words at Gethsemane — "Only as Thy will is, not as mine is"[78] — mean something quite different. We find none of those periods of fatigue and reinvigoration, resistance and abandon. Nothing of the sort. Jesus was no prophet.

As we have said before, everything Jesus says, He possesses. The God of whom He speaks is within Him. Now we must look more closely and say the following: Jesus does not speak from hearsay, nor as having received His message from somewhere. He speaks from essence itself. He is different from the believer, and therefore He does not speak as the believer speaks. If we listen with true attention to the way He speaks about God, how He announces and commands, we find ourselves in the presence of an interior mystery quite other than the mystery of a believer, or a prophet: we are in the mystery of the God-Man.

[77] Matt. 3:16-17; Mark 1:9-11; Luke 3:21-22.
[78] Matt. 26:42; Luke 22:42.

Chapter Seven

How to Satisfy the Deepest Hunger of All

My food is to do the will
of Him who sent me.
John 4:34

We get a more profound insight into the nature of our Lord if we contemplate the significance of His Father's will in His life.

The twelve-year-old boy sitting in the temple was asked by His frightened mother, "My Son, why hast Thou treated us so? Think what anguish of mind Thy father and I have endured, searching for Thee!" And He answered with the astonishment of one taking something for granted: "What reason had you to search for me? Could you not tell that I must be in the place which belongs to my Father?"[79] Already in the boy there is an interior "I must." He had no need to reflect, "Should I do this or that?" It was: "I must." There was a deep-seated drive in Him, which did not derive from a willed intent; it led Him, carried Him on, so that all action stemmed from inner necessity, a necessity, however, that does not preclude freedom, but rather so orders things that the free act proceeds from the ultimate core of identity. The author of this necessity is the will of the Father.

After Jesus was baptized in the Jordan, we read, He was led by the Holy Spirit into the desert: "Immediately the Spirit drove Him into the desert"[80] — so says Mark with prophetic

[79] Luke 2:48-49.
[80] Mark 1:12.

violence. Force works upon Him; illumination, compulsion, inspiration. This power, too, is the will of the Father, but under the form of the *pneuma*, the Spirit, which is the love of the Father. We expect to find that same overwhelming force which seized Elijah, Elisha, Habakkuk, and Daniel, turning the simple figure of a man into God's instrument.

Jesus spoke in Capernaum. All were deeply moved and satisfied; they entreated Him to remain. But He would not, saying, "Let us go to the next country towns, so that I can preach there, too; it is for this that I have come."[81] Jesus knew that He was not acting from private judgment and volition, but that He was the one who had been sent. A commission lives in Him. Carrying out this commission is the content of His life. Everything serves to that end. Everything is thereby made legitimate. And this mission is, again, the will of the Father.

One day, wandering through Samaria, all weary, He sat down at Jacob's Well. The disciples went on to the town to buy food for their meal. A woman came up to the well, and He held that memorable conversation with her concerning the new era that was now upon them, in which it was not to be upon this mountain nor that one, but "in spirit and in truth" that God was meant to be worshiped. The disciples returned: "Master, take some food!" Then He answered them as if from a long way off: "I have food to eat of which you know nothing." Puzzled and uncomprehending, they asked one another, "Can somebody have brought Him food?" But He said, "My food is to do the will of Him who sent me."[82]

[81] Mark 1:38.
[82] John 4:5-34.

To hunger and thirst is the deepest need man is capable of expressing. It is part of our very nature to be hungry — hungry for that which will satisfy us for eternity. Using this elemental human need as a figure of speech, Jesus was saying that it stilled His hunger to do the will of the Father. And this was no mere allegory, indeed not, but something lived. His being hungered for the realization of His Father's will, driving from within, demanding fulfillment.

Another passage is perhaps even more basic to this discussion. Jesus was sitting inside a house talking to the people about Him. They told Him, "Behold, Thy mother and brethren are without, looking for Thee." And He, who knew so well who His mother was, answered from the very depths of which He drew His life, "Who is a mother, who are brethren, to me?" And looking over the circle of people about Him, He said: "If anyone does the will of God, he is my brother and sister and mother."[83]

We must not allow these words to be interpreted as allegory, or probed psychologically anymore than the foregoing ones. The will of the Father is reality. It is like a river of life coming down from the Father to Christ — a lifestream from which he draws life, even more profoundly, more truly, and more powerfully than He draws life from His mother. And whoever is ready to do the will of the Father becomes a part of this lifestream, and this will then pulses through him from the heart of the Father, and he is united to the life of Christ more truly, more deeply, and more strongly than the way in which Christ was united to His mother.

[83] Mark 3:32-35.

The will of the Father is most precious, the very highest, so that He gives care and concern for it to those who belong to Him. That God's will be done is the concern of the Christian. It is expressed in the Lord's Prayer, and should be expressed in the Christian's whole attitude toward life.

This will of the Father is a power in Jesus, a satisfying of hunger, a fulfillment; but it is no coercion. The Father's will does not bind in a spell. There is no question of hypnotic suggestion, no forcible constraint, and no being pushed and bent without any proper will. The will of the Father speaks to Jesus, and in His freedom, He receives it.

We can share this experience in that darkest hour when He is in Gethsemane, face-to-face with this will in all the terror of what it requires of Him: "My Father, if it is possible, let this chalice pass from me. Nevertheless, not as I will, but as Thou wilt."[84] This is the encounter of the two Persons: no spell, no dark and compelling force is at work here, but rather an appeal and a comprehension. It is so much so that it is expressed in the form of a contradiction: "Not as I will, *but* as Thou wilt" — from there to come together in the deepest, holiest unity, in which the will of the Father is completely taken up in His own; His will ascends completely into the will of the Father.

And it is like a last, beatific expression of His interior life when He says, "I will always do the will of my Father."[85] This enables us to look deeply into the interior nature of Jesus. His Father's will is the source from which He draws life. His

[84] Matt. 26:39 (Douay-Rheims edition).
[85] Cf. John 8:29.

Father's will is that mighty, impelling force from which His every act proceeds as if by necessity. This is the great power of the *pneuma*, which fills Jesus and guides Him. His Father's will is the command living within Jesus which makes of Him one who was sent, and everything He does draws purpose and unity therefrom. His Father's will is the food which satisfies the hunger within Him. It is the lifestream pulsing through Him, and whosoever binds himself to follow this same will of the Father is caught up in this stream. The most precious thing of all is this will, the substance of the deepest and most delicate concern. But in all of this, there is no question of constraint — the surrender of one will to the mastery of another. Rather, it is an appeal from one Person to Another, realized in perfect freedom.

The Lord's entire life proceeds from His Father's will. But it is in this wise that He is truly Himself. He is truly Himself in that He does not do His own will, but the will of His Father, and so fulfills the deepest and most private principle of His being. There is a word for this: love.

His Father's will is the Father's love. In His will, the Father comes to Jesus in person. His appeals, His orders and commands are a "coming." And in accepting this will, Jesus receives the Father. Addressing this will and its fulfillment is the generous acceptance of this love. It is only from this point on that words take on the sense of "must," the "food," the lifestream, concern for fulfillment, "Not my will, but Thine"; and the beatific triumph of the words "The will of my Father I shall do always."

We would feel an exaggeration, an overdriving, a forcible upheaval, were we only to consider this will objectively, as a moral imperative of righteousness or whatever. But one can only receive something from such a source as this into the interior life, the heart and the spirit, if what is received is love.

If we listen hence to the inner Jesus vibrating through all His deeds and sayings, we can always sense a continuing interior dialogue; it is always the Father who says, "Do this"; and Jesus answers, "Yes, I will; all is well." An encounter and a unity of spirit are there at one and the same time. There is a divine blessedness here.

Chapter Eight

∞

Why Jesus Was
Abandoned by All

Behold, the time is coming . . .
when you . . . shall
leave me alone.
John 16:32

Once before in the course of these meditations, when we were speaking of our Lord as being in a state of passage through the world, we mentioned His solitude. Understanding this takes us so intimately into the heart of His mystery that we shall examine it again.

We assume today, almost as a matter of course, that a person of exceptional greatness of character, with the penetration and the creative gift of genius, is slated to be misunderstood in his own lifetime — so much so that we feel Providence is being kind whenever such a person finds recognition before it is too late. Consider one whose condition in life comprises factors far beyond the general run of mankind, to begin with; whose background and destiny have formed him in a special way; who has broken through to new knowledge by the road of searching analyses and extraordinary experiences of the inner life, touched by values not yet apprehended by the rest of mankind, seeing goals and possibilities hitherto concealed from others. Such a person simply cannot expect any kind of immediate reception by the general public. In a favorable situation, he may be surrounded by a certain respect, but he must go his way alone. In an unfavorable situation, he will encounter mistrust or hostility. Of course, afterward, when he has fought his fight, possibly perished, then the people take him and his followers to their bosom. Then he appears as the messenger and prophet of what is later seen to be the commonweal.

Such is not the case with Jesus. We must not think of His life in this category so familiar to history. He was not just another great man misunderstood in his own time. It went much deeper than that.

Let us just reflect upon this: Jesus was a Jew. He came of the finest stock of His people, the line of kings. He was wholly rooted in the life of this people. It has been said, and with some justice, that His immediate humanity is even today most readily understood by the Jews. He was deeply involved in the tradition of His people. Their whole history lived in Him. He knew Himself to be deeply obligated to this sacred record. Suffused as He was by the tremendous mission received directly from God, He said, "Do not think that I have come to set aside the law and the prophets; I have not come to set them aside, but to bring them to perfection." Not one letter, no "jot" or "tittle" may be taken away;[86] everything must be fulfilled.

More than that: He knew how the purpose of His being, and His mission was borne out by that sacred past. "You pore over the Scriptures, thinking to find eternal life in them; and indeed it is of these I speak as bearing witness to me."[87] Those events had now demonstrated their place in the order of things. The entire Old Testament was directed toward a future, to be fulfilled by waiting for something that was to come, the Messiah, and the kingdom of God, which the Messiah was

---

[86] Matt. 5:17, 18.
[87] John 5:39.

to bring about. Jesus puts Himself in this very place; He was the one referred to there.

The first time He spoke in His home synagogue, it is about this text: "The Spirit of the Lord is upon me; He has anointed me, and sent me out to preach the gospel to the poor, to restore the broken-hearted; to bid the prisoners to go free and the blind to have sight; to set the oppressed at liberty, to proclaim a year when men may find acceptance with the Lord." And He begins with the words "This scripture which I have read in your hearing is today fulfilled."[88]

When John sent his messengers to ask Him, "Is it Thy coming that was foretold, or are we yet waiting for some other?" He answered with the words of the messianic prophecy of Isaiah: "Go and tell John what your own eyes have witnessed: how the blind see, and the lame walk, and the lepers are made clean, and the deaf hear; how the dead are raised to life, and the poor have the gospel preached to them. Blessed is he who does not lose confidence in me."[89]

And what did His people do? They did not receive Him. They refused Him; they turned away from Him. They eradicated Him.

This happened not only because it has always been thus with men sent by God. Almost all of the prophets were rejected or persecuted by their own people, but thereafter they were all the more passionately revered in their person and for their message. After two thousand years, Jesus continues to be rejected.

---

[88] Luke 4:18-21.
[89] Luke 7:20-23; Isa. 35:5-6.

How did that happen?

There is nothing unusual in the fact that mistrust and enmity very soon began to mingle with enthusiasm, for this is common in the affairs of men. However, it is quite remarkable to contemplate with what spontaneous agreement the opposition formed against Him. The mistrustful staring figures lurked about Him as if in ambush and very soon began deciding how best to destroy His effectiveness. There is no mention of any real attack on His claims or His teachings. There is no passage to the effect that they came up to Him and said, "You claim that You were sent: on what do You base such a claim? You have performed certain acts by way of a sign to support these claims: show us what this is supposed to prove. You identify Yourself with the expectation of a Messiah: how do You place Yourself with the figure of the Messiah as it stands in Isaiah, Jeremiah, Malachi, and all the rest? You criticize so much about us: tell us, what is Your basis for all this criticism? You are bringing something special, something new: tell us in what relation this thing stands with the old."

There was nothing of that sort. The battle was joined immediately. One might remark that this kind of dispute is not apt to be conducted very objectively. True enough. But then it becomes clear just what the opposition meant — namely, how they apprehended this tremendous phenomenon, and how, from the first moment on, there was no frankness, no disposition toward understanding, not even a readiness to engage in a serious argument. In a short time, the blank wall of their refusal to understand — their disowning — closed in, and the wall grew ever harder and ever narrower, until it crushed Him.

He also had fundamentally the same experience with the people. At first they took Him up with high enthusiasm. They hungered for His bread, for His words, for His healing power; they followed Him and wanted to make Him king. However, in John's Gospel, we find that penetrating, realistic phrase: "But Jesus would not give them His confidence . . . because He could read men's hearts."[90] They did not understand what He was driving at, nor had they any intuition of the heart concerning Him. The people, too, made a wall between themselves and Him: the impenetrable heaviness and slothfulness of their hearts.

We have several times made mention of Jesus' disciples. They were with Him throughout. They had indeed all come to Him in an open-hearted fashion; they heard the words He spoke and saw what He did. They saw Him, no less!

If we, too, could only see Him once walking down the street! To see His face while he spoke, or a movement of His hand. If we could only hear His voice, catch the tone of it, the special way He spoke! Only to hear such a thing, might we not well be changed into quite different people? We might expect the sight of an expression on His face to invade our very hearts, burn itself in.

Jesus' disciples possessed all these things, pressed down and flowing over, and yet they did not understand Him.

The Gospels tell us over and over that the disciples did not understand Him — and we must not forget that these Gospels were written by the disciples themselves, and with the help of insight from the later period, so they are truly trustworthy in spite of themselves when they say, "They did not understand

---

[90] John 2:24-25.

Him." It says in Luke's Gospel, "But they could not under-stand what He said; it was hidden from them, so they could not perceive the meaning of it"; and what follows makes their lack of understanding even more hopeless: "And they were afraid to ask Him about this saying of His."[91]

Such a misconception of the magnitude of His mission, the kingdom of God! They tried to draw it down into the mun-dane, political order. And even at the very last moment, after the tremendous events of the Passion and the Resurrection had taken place, right on the very same Mount of Olives where it had all begun, they misunderstood Him again: "Lord, dost Thou mean to restore the dominion to Israel here and now?"[92] Is the glory finally at hand?

Our Lord never saw the day when their spirits would open up and understand what He wanted, when their hearts might receive the impact of His will and pass it on. Everything always remains narrow, heavy, petty, and barren. Their lack of under-standing even reached the grotesque at the time they were on board ship crossing the lake to Capernaum after the multipli-cation of the loaves. Jesus was still dwelling inwardly on what He had done and the events just past. Suddenly, as from the depths of His being, He warned them, "Look well, and avoid the leaven of the Pharisees, and the leaven of Herod!" They still had bread and bake-shops on their minds, and said anx-iously to one another, "He is saying that because we have brought no bread." And Jesus, as if in an outburst from the tor-ment within Him, said, "What is this anxiety that you have

[91] Luke 9:45.
[92] Acts 1:6.

brought no bread with you? Have you no sense, no wits, even now? Is your heart still dull?"[93] Once again the wall was rising up around Him, and from a quarter that must have oppressed His humanity worst of all — those closest to Him.

What about His family, what of them? How revealing is that passage in John's Gospel where Jesus' brethren say to Him, " 'This is no place for Thee; go to Judea, so that Thy disciples also may see Thy doings. Nobody is content to act in secret, if he wishes to make himself known at large; if Thou must act thus, show Thyself before the world!' For even His brethren were without faith in Him."[94]

We must bear in mind one passage about His mother and Joseph, bound to Him by such affection. "These words which He spoke to them were beyond their understanding."[95] It is true the passage continues: "His mother kept in her heart the memory of all this"[96] — precious seed that was later to grow into purest recognition of love, when the Holy Spirit had descended upon her too. But for the time being, matters stood at the hard saying, "beyond their understanding."

Jesus remained in a state of inexpressible isolation.

John, who had rested on His bosom, the only one of the disciples who, although he, too, had fled, pulled himself together and came back and stood the painful watch beneath the Cross. He had understood the inner Jesus better than any. His Gospel is our key to this: it is also the key to the whole

---

[93] Mark 8:14-17.
[94] John 7:3-5.
[95] Luke 2:50.
[96] Luke 2:51.

New Testament. But his Gospel and letters are quite staggered by the unfathomable quality of this mystery, how such things could be, how the Lord had come into the world which had come into being through Him, and which received Him not.

Let us once more project ourselves imaginatively into what it must mean when a man is full of the profoundest insight into what is necessary for everyone's salvation, full of the purest sort of love, ready to open his heart, to offer himself, and to be of help. And then he comes and speaks to one, and to another, and he encounters distrust here and incomprehension there, mocking laughter, and hostility — this is what Jesus had to go through. And it was so much worse than that: ungodly, dreadful! He carried within Himself the truth which came from God. He was bringing with that immeasurable healing power which could say, "Come unto me, all of you, and I will refresh you."[97] He knew how things stood with people and the world, and He had the power to remove the very foundations of distress. But everywhere He ran up against a blank wall. Such suffering as this indeed must been terrible.

But the worst of it was that it never let up; the darkness never gave way to light; the closed hearts never opened the least bit. Instead, everything only grew flintier, more obscure than before, more hostile, right up to the "hour of the powers of darkness."[98]

This gives us some conception of what sin is, and the Fall of creation, to have such a thing be possible as this blindness and hardening of hearts! We also get some idea of what Redemption

[97] Matt. 11:28.
[98] Luke 22:53.

means: He had to suffer all this misery until the very end in order to pay the price of sin. He bore with this state of being immured within Himself, of being refused by those He had come to redeem — bore it without escape or relief until death. If we arrive at an understanding of this ultimate, most pregnant, most inexorable fact in our hearts, we will have understood something of what the Redemption is about. He could only have been able to endure it by that mystery which John repeatedly mentions: "The Father is with me always."[99]

But solitude, isolation, penetrated even here. The same Gospel tells of Jesus crying out in His last agony, "My God, my God, why hast Thou forsaken me?"[100]

In the final fulfillment of the redeeming oblation, in the blackest darkness of the doom of death, even the nearness of the Father withdrew, and He was left quite alone.

[99] John 16:32.
[100] Matt. 27:46.

Chapter Nine

∞

The Nearness of
Our Heavenly Father

The Father is with me.
John 16:32

We have reflected on the solitude of Jesus: how He stood alone against the responsible leaders of His people, who did not understand Him, and even turned Him away, and took action against Him; how He stood alone among His people, who, it is true, cheered for Him for a short time, but afterward abandoned Him; how He stood alone even among His disciples, the closest to Him of all, who lived with Him, for these neither understood Him nor kept faith with Him, except for John.

And when we asked ourselves what He had to hold on to through all this, we ran across the profoundly interior sentence from the message of farewell: "And yet I am not alone, because the Father is with me."[101] Jesus' solitude becomes something frightful and incomprehensible if we do not understand it in connection with the presence of His Father.

When Jesus speaks of the heavenly Father, our attention is drawn to a particular detail which discloses a great deal: in His relationship to the Father, He never includes Himself together with those He summons. He teaches us to say the Our Father; therein are we to be bound to one another and united. But He never mentions this word in connection with Himself

[101] John 16:32.

and us together; He always says, "My Father," "your Father."[102] This alone indicates that His relation to the Father was a special one.

Often the Gospel story tells that He left the circle of the disciples and the people around Him to go into solitude, on a mountain or to some quiet place. At such times, He was with His Father, and received the message of His will, and received Him into His heart.

We may look into one of these colloquies, the one that took place on Gethsemane, where He learned the final will of His Father and surrendered Himself to it.

John is the one who illuminates for us the interior life of Jesus, the most private of His feelings and that depth of nature which placed Him so far above all created things. In the words of farewell spoken by Jesus to His disciples the evening before His death, this profundity is especially evident. He spoke at this time of the will of His Father, and of His commandment: "I have bestowed my love upon you, just as my Father has bestowed His love upon me; live on, then, in my love. You will live on in my love if you keep my commandments, just as it is by keeping my Father's commandments that I live on in His love."[103] We feel the presence in those words. The commandment, the will of the Father is no impersonal rule taken from somewhere. The Father Himself is His will; and that means His commandment is love. And when Jesus receives the Father's will, He is "in the Father's love," the Father is with Him, and there is a unity there whence springs peace, *His* peace.

---

[102] John 20:17.
[103] John 15:9-10.

The Nearness of Our Heavenly Father

In Chapter 14 of John's Gospel, we find Jesus speaking once again of this holy intermingling of commandment and love and the presence of His Father: "It is only a little while now, before the world is to see me no more; but you can see me, because I live on, and you, too, will have life. When that day comes, you will learn for yourselves that I am in my Father, and you are in me, and I am in you. The man who loves me is the man who keeps the commandments he has from me; and he who loves me will win my Father's love, and I, too, will love him, and will reveal myself to him."[104]

There is a close fellowship between Jesus and the Father: standing in readiness to open up and include whoever enters into the mystery of the will of God.

We read further, "If a man has any love for me, he will be true to my word; and then he will win my Father's love, and we will both come to him, and make our continual abode with him; whereas the man who has no love for me lets my sayings pass him by. And this word, which you have been hearing from me, comes not from me, but from my Father, who sent me."[105]

This, I believe, is the first time in the New Testament that the sacred word *We*, the Father and Jesus, appears. But His word and His commandment to the disciples only pass along the word and the commandment the Father directed to Him.

Whosoever stands obedient to the love of Jesus enters into the mystery of the nearness which binds the Lord to the Father. And full of blessed overflowing fulfillment are those words: "We will both come to him, and make our continual abode

[104] John 14:19-21.
[105] John 14:23-24.

85

with him." Jesus lives in the presence of the Father. This proximity is brought about by the Father's will and Jesus' obedience. There is a unison of love in this nearness; and in this unison, there is joy and the most ineffable peace.

In the same chapter we find: "Peace is my bequest to you, and the peace which I give you is mine to give; I do not give peace as the world gives it. Do not let your hearts be distressed or play the coward. You have heard me say that I am going away and coming back to you. If you really loved me, you would be glad to hear that I am on my way to my Father; my Father has greater power than I."[106]

It is not just peace in general, not just some sort of harmony; it is the peace of Christ — that peace which cannot be given by any created thing; that peace which consists in the unity of love between Jesus and the Father, and in Jesus' surrender to His Will. This peace is what the Father gives to anyone who opens himself to receive Him. In this fashion, the believer takes part in that unity. Jesus, who went up to the Father and is secure with Him, "comes" into it; and He brings that unity, and that presence, and gives them to man for his very own.

The presence of His Father is so close to our Lord, and His oneness with Him such an interior thing, that the living Jesus Christ is simply the Father become visible. We read, " 'And although I do go to prepare you a home, I am coming back; and then I will take you to myself, so that you, too, may be where I am. And now you, too, know where it is I am going; and you know the way there.' Thomas said to Him, 'But, Lord, we do

---

[106] John 14:27-28.

not know where Thou art going; how are we to know the way there?' Jesus said to him, 'I am the way; I am truth and life; nobody can come to the Father, except through me. If you had learned to recognize me, you would have learned to recognize my Father, too. From now onward you are to recognize Him; you have seen Him.' At this Philip said to Him, 'Lord, let us see the Father; that is all we ask.' 'What, Philip,' Jesus said to him, 'here am I, who have been all this while in your company; hast thou not learned to recognize me yet? Whoever has seen me has seen the Father; what dost thou mean by saying, "Let us see the Father"? Do you not believe that I am in the Father, and the Father is in me?' "[107]

The true and substantial proximity of the Father is enjoyed only by Christ. There is no direct communication between us and the Father. He dwells in mystery, and only the Son is "in Him." Therefore the Father's nearness, as promised to us, can be only through Christ. He is the way, the truth, and the life, and no one comes to the Father except by Him.

But if we ask, "Who is the Father? What sort of Father is He? What does He look like?" Jesus gives us the answer: "Whoever has seen me, has seen the Father." The presence, so evident within and about Jesus; the great one present from whom Jesus draws life and toward whom He is directed, concerning whom He brings tidings, to whom He addresses Himself, whose will He performs, and from whose bonds comes His peace — that is the Father.

It did not happen that man discovered and recognized God the Father by his own efforts and that Christ came along

[107] John 14:3-10.

afterward and told us profounder things about Him. The Father we have been called to believe in, from whom our salvation comes, where the "everlasting dwellings"[108] are, is "God and Father of Jesus Christ,"[109] plain and visible in Him.

Jesus' loneliness while in the world was unutterable. His final words of farewell to the disciples reveal how dreadful this loneliness was.

John's Gospel reads, " 'It was from the Father that I came, when I entered the world, and now I am leaving the world, and going on my way to the Father.' Hereupon His disciples said to Him, 'Why, now Thou art speaking openly enough; this is no parable Thou art uttering. Now we can be sure that Thou knowest all things, not needing to wait until Thou art asked; this gives us faith that Thou wast sent by God.' 'You have faith, now?' Jesus answered. 'Behold, the time is coming — no, has already come — when you are to be scattered, each of you taking his own path, and to leave me alone. And yet I am not alone, because the Father is with me.' "[110]

We have to listen closely to the echo of these sentences; they have a sound of coming from an immense distance. He is telling them that He will no longer speak to them in images, but will henceforth openly give testimony of the Father. The disciples hear this, and with a momentary flash of sensitivity, as if light had come to their understanding, they say, "Now you are talking straightforwardly! Now you aren't using images! Now we know that you know everything, and we believe that

[108] Luke 16:9.
[109] Rom. 15:6.
[110] John 16:28-32.

you come from God." But Jesus answered them with all the pitiless clarity of his position: "Behold, the time is coming — no, has already come — when you are to be scattered, each of you taking his own path, and to leave me alone."

This very moment, when they think they understand Him, He knows well there is no understanding there, and no fidelity, and no interior intimacy. Soon He will be alone in an external sense as well. At this moment, words are spoken from the deepest ties that bind Him: "And yet I am not alone, because the Father is with me."

Our meditation by now has traveled far. We have been attempting, each time from a different point of view, to penetrate into the mystery of the Lord. Now we have arrived at the core of the mystery.

When Jesus turns back within Himself, He encounters the Father. When Jesus takes counsel with Himself, it is the Father's word He hears. When He directs His ear to the present moment, the Father's will addresses itself to Him. And this will is the Father Himself; and in hearkening to this will, Jesus is united in filial love with His Father.

Jesus' meat and drink is to do the will of the Father. Jesus' life is to be according to this will. His joy and His peace are in being near the presence of His Father. But it is not just a question of close presence, but unity.

Chapter Ten

How Jesus Lifts Us into Eternity

Before Abraham ever
came to be, I am.
John 8:58

∞

Our meditations have attempted to drive ever deeper into the mystery of Christ. We have spoken of the visible figure of His person, of the mystery that surrounded Him, of His healing the sick, and of the purpose behind it; of His solitude, how He stood always encompassed by the Father's will, and of how close He was to the Father. Now we are to try to say the last things which are to be said.

To hear the decisive word on what sort of man Jesus was, one must turn to John. The other evangelists, too, have marvelous things to tell about Him. What they tell has a quality of pure contemporaneousness, of intimate heartfelt closeness to the subject. They were the first to commit their accounts to writing, and they give the impression closest in time to the events they describe.

But is the closest view always the most complete? Is it the one that goes deepest? When a man of thirty looks back on his childhood, and a man of sixty looks back at his, which of the two sees more, penetrates deeper with his vision, encompasses with the more powerful understanding that essence of childhood in all its special atmosphere of beginnings and its particular texture?

The writers of the Synoptic Gospels looked deeply into Jesus, but the ultimate revelation was made only by John. He wrote as an old man, out of the fullness of Christian experience and the perfection of his own interior life. He looked backward with the penetrating, highly associative perception of mature memory; and he was the "disciple whom Jesus loved,"[111] who had laid his head on Jesus' breast and, as it says in the Liturgy, "drank the everlasting waters streaming therefrom." He has the last word to say on the Master.

His entire Gospel speaks of the inner mystery of the Lord. We shall select some of these Gospel sayings for quotation here. They are intended — as is everything in these meditations — to encourage us to look, on our own initiative, more deeply into the fullness of the Gospels.

On one occasion — it is reported after the episode with the woman taken in adultery — Jesus said to the Pharisees, "I am the Light of the World. He who follows me can never walk in darkness; he will possess the light which is life."[112]

What a mighty phrase! "I am the Light of the World." Let us imagine ourselves saying the same thing, at a time when we feel how particularly confused our existence has become, when we are proceeding in darkness, without knowing whence or whither, happy if we can even see as far as the next step we are to take. Then we have some measure of what it means for someone to stand and say, "I am the Light of the World." For He is maintaining nothing less than that everything within Him is clear, everything about Him is clear: no confusion, no deceit; that He sees clearly, judges aright, and can look ahead over cause, goal, and the relationship between these things.

[111] John 21:20.
[112] John 8:12.

But He says not simply, "I am bright" or "shining," but, "I am *the* Light"; and even more: "the Light of the World," that is, the Light the World needs — all things, everyone, all men, all creatures. The Light to light the way to reach salvation, to come to God: that is what He is! When some people have to follow a path in the black of night, and one of them has a lantern, this is then their light; if it goes out, they are in darkness. And so is He the Light, the only one there is for all the world.

Such a word as this is enough to strike terror into one's heart.

In the farewell, Jesus told His disciples that He was going away, and that they knew the path He would travel. Thomas said to Him, "But, Lord, we do not know where Thou art going; how are we to know the way there?" And Jesus said to him, "I am the way; I am truth and life. Nobody can come to the Father except through me."[113]

Once again we must weigh these words. Jesus does not say, "I will show you the way," but rather "I *am* the way"; not "I will teach you the truth," but rather "I *am* the truth"; not "I bring you life," but "I *am* life." This is not said by way of rhetorical exaggeration, but rather with intense awareness of exactly what is involved. There was no path already there, which Jesus simply pointed out; or a general truth already in existence, to which He merely called attention; or a wellspring of the abundant life, which He made to gush forth. Nor was it a matter of there being already present a living relationship with God, plain for all to see, with His mission nothing more than to make it easier of access. The way, the truth, and the life, union

[113] John 14:4-6.

with the living God: these are He. No one comes to the Father except through Him.

If someone should ask, "How do I come to God? What kind of being is God?" this would be the answer: God is just as He manifested Himself in Jesus. Whoever looks upon Jesus, whoever takes into account who Jesus is, how He speaks, how He conducts Himself, what His attitudes are — such a one is perceiving God Himself. And he will get to God by going in Jesus' company, allowing himself to be instructed by Him, and allowing himself to become centered in that identity with which he makes his approach to Jesus. Then he is indeed on the way, in truth, and he partakes of life.

"It was on the feast of the Dedication of the Temple . . . and Jesus was walking up and down Solomon's Porch. The Jews gathered around him, and said to Him, 'How long wilt Thou go on keeping us in suspense? If Thou art the Christ, tell us openly.' Jesus answered them, 'I have told you, but you will not believe me. All that I do in my Father's name bears me testimony, and still you will not believe me; that is because you are no sheep of mine. My sheep listen to my voice, and I know them, and they follow me. And I give them everlasting life, so that to all eternity they can never be lost; no one can tear them away from the hand of my Father. My Father and I are one.' "[114]

"My Father and I are *one*." That word means something tremendous, and is intended to be so understood. For immediately thereafter we read, "The Jews once again took up stones, to stone him with."[115] This people, formed in the school of the

---

[114] John 10:22-30.
[115] John 10:31.

prophets to recognize the sound and the implication of words on religion — jealous guardians of the purity of their belief in God, for which they had been suffering and warring for a thousand years — hear a possibility of blasphemy: "It is not for any deed of mercy that we are stoning Thee; it is for blasphemy. It is because Thou, who art a man, dost pretend to be God!"[116]

But Jesus takes nothing back, gives no ground: "Is it not written in your law, 'I have said, "You are gods"'? He gave the title of gods to those who had God's message sent to them; and we know that the words of Scripture have binding force. Why then, what of Him whom God has sanctified and sent into the world? Will you call me a blasphemer because I have told you I am the Son of God?"[117] Now it is no more just the condition of being the sons of God because the Jews were a Chosen People, sometimes called "sons of God"; no longer merely sons of God in the order of grace, which is promised to any believer. Nor does it even mean the elevation of a uniquely great individual as the "servant of God." Much more is now here. Here is an utterance which insists on a clear choice: outright blasphemy or something else — something hitherto unheard.

Once He addressed those Jews who had come to believe in Him: "If you continue faithful to my word, you are my disciples in earnest; so you will come to know the truth, and the truth will set you free." Instantly pride and hurt feelings raged within them. They answered Him, "We are of Abraham's breed; nobody ever enslaved us. What dost Thou mean by saying, 'You

[116]John 10:33.
[117]John 10:34-36.

shall become free'?" Jesus marked how evil was gathering within them and said, "If you are Abraham's true children, it is for you to follow Abraham's example. As it is, you are designing to kill me, who tell you the truth as I have heard it from God. This was not Abraham's way."[118]

Remark and repartee become very rough at this point. We can feel the hardness of heart returning in these who are almost believers, until finally He flings in their face: "You belong to your father, that is, the Devil, and are eager to gratify the appetites which are your father's. He, from the first, was a murderer." Then they say, "We are right, surely, in saying that Thou art a Samaritan, and art possessed?"

And Jesus replies, "Believe me when I tell you this; if a man is true to my word, to all eternity, he will never see death." The Jews say, "Now we are certain that Thou art possessed. What of Abraham and the prophets? They are dead; and Thou sayest that a man will never taste death to all eternity, if he is true to Thy word. Art Thou greater than our father Abraham? He is dead, and the prophets are dead. What dost Thou claim to be?"

And Jesus answers, "If I should speak in my own honor, such honor goes for nothing. Honor must come to me from my Father, whom you claim as your God; although you cannot recognize Him. But I have knowledge of Him; if I should say I have not, I should be what you are, a liar. Yes, I have knowledge of Him, am true to His word. As for your father Abraham, his heart was proud to see the day of my coming; he saw, and rejoiced to see it." Then the Jews say to Him, "Hast

[118] John 8:31-33, 39-40.

Thou seen Abraham, Thou, who art not yet fifty years old?"
And Jesus says, "Believe me, before Abraham ever came to be,
I am."[119]

The Lord spoke such words only once. It was like a sudden
ray of eternity shining. "Believe me, before Abraham ever
came to be, I am." Abraham had lived a thousand years before,
yet before Abraham was born — not "I was" (time is in this
concept), but rather "I am." The long history of the Jewish
people was past and gone, and what happened before that goes
back into the mists of darkness. A long history of mankind is
to follow, no one knows for how long: the one is past; the other
is to come. Here stood someone, born of His mother in Bethlehem, thirty years before. And now, death close at hand, this
someone says, "Before Abraham ever came to be, I am." Eternal consciousness appears within time: the consciousness of
everlasting being.

Here, in the living inwardness of Jesus, the path is opened
to that secret, the figure that overshadows what is reported in
the beginning of St. John's Gospel, where it reads, "At the beginning of time, the Word already was; and God had the Word
abiding with Him, and the Word was God. He abode, at the
beginning of time, with God. It was through Him that all
things came into being, and without Him came nothing that
has come to be. In Him there was life, and that life was the light
of men. And the light shines in darkness, a darkness which
was not able to master it."

And then: "And the Word was made flesh, and came to
dwell among us; and we had sight of His glory, glory such as

[119] John 8:44, 52-58.

belongs to the Father's only-begotten Son, full of grace and truth."[120]

And at the beginning of his first letter, St. John declares, "Our message concerns that Word, who is life." And it continues like an echo of the foregoing: ". . . what He was from the first, what we have heard about Him, what our eyes have seen of Him; what it was that met our gaze and the touch of our hands. Yes, life dawned; and it is as eyewitnesses that we give you news of that life, that eternal life, which ever abode with the Father and has dawned, now, on us. This message about what we have seen and heard we pass on to you, so that you, too, may share our fellowship."[121]

"Before Abraham ever came to be, I am." That sentence announced His eternity. It becomes apparent now who He is: the Word. He is the Word that has been uttered. He is the living fullness of the being and truth of God, spoken by God, who is the Father in the actual substantive Word; He is the Word that is with God the Father, with the one who speaks, and at the same time the Word addressed to the speaker, by way of answer from His coexistent Son.

And this Word is truly God. All things are created in Him. All meaning, all value, all truth, and all the fact of being derives from Him. He is the Light of the World, and the life thereof.

This is the last thing said, and everything depends on not merely taking it in superficially, but hearkening to it prayerfully and in awe.

[120] John 1:1-5, 14.
[121] 1 John 1:1-3.

If a man goes back into himself, he finds a man. If I look within myself, I find my thoughts, my excitements, my guilt, my sorrow, and the entire distress and poverty of my finiteness. I find myself. But when Jesus called upon Himself — the "I" who answered within Him was God. And God was also the one who called.

The nearness of the Father was not just the nearness of grace, and the condition of having been chosen. It was that nearness binding the Father to the eternal Word, which He speaks, and which is directed to Him. The Father's will, by which Jesus lived, was not, as with the prophets, heard from a far-off Lord and Creator. In His will, the Father came to Him and was with Him: "I and the Father are one."

His sense of aloneness among the rest of men sprang from this being one with the Father, for He was different from them. And at the same time, He was able to endure this isolation because of this very oneness. This is where the power of His healing and His help shines forth, brought into play not only by His humanity, but to make plain the way which leads to the Father.

From this aspect mystery blew about Him, and made people feel drawn to Him, yet at the same time, afraid of Him. This was the true seal and imprint of His person. This was the mark showing that He was only passing through this world, coming from the Father and going back to Him. This made it right for His passage through this world to be a failure from the worldly point of view; for if it is true that, the nobler and more precious a thing is, the weaker it must be in this difficult and violent world, then this must be true twice over in His case. If God really became man, living not as a miraculous being — Satan tempted Him in this way at the beginning of His ministry — but rather as a true person, "like us in all things except sin,"[122] then this God become man, become flesh, had to be the weakest thing in this world.

Not without meaning was it said that God "emptied Himself,"[123] made Himself into nothing, abandoned His consciousness, when He came into the world. When God became man, He entered into the condition of a sacrificial victim.

[122] Heb. 4:15.
[123] Phil. 2:7.

Chapter Eleven

How We Can Experience Christ's Boundless Love

He still loved those who
were His own, whom He
was leaving in the world.
John 13:1

In our last meditation, we came to that most interior part of Jesus' identity. We contemplated that mystery that shines forth each time Jesus said, "I"; when He encountered other men; when He acted, and experienced destiny. And now we will dwell on Jesus' love.

He was the greatest Lover. In the first letter of St. John, we read, "God is love."[124] This might have been said of Jesus Himself, and it would still be the same: Jesus is love.

Love proceeded from Him everywhere. We encounter love all around Him. But we want to seek it out in the flaming, radiant center. Love is what He shows toward the delicate blossoming of His Father's creation, when He speaks of the lilies of the field, and how God has clothed them more magnificently than Solomon in all his glory. He shows love toward all things living and breathing when He speaks of the birds of the air — light, free of worry, who toil not, and yet the Father in Heaven feeds them.[125]

This kind of love is indeed beautiful. But love of this same sort may be found among others, even better expressed, more highly colored, and more from the heart. Consider St. Francis

[124] 1 John 4:8.
[125] Matt. 6:28-30, 26.

of Assisi[126] who called everything in this world brother and sister.

Love is what seizes our Lord when He sees the obscure, abandoned masses of the people, and takes pity on them because they are like sheep that have no shepherd.[127] There is something heroic, strong, in this love for people forsaken and in distress. But others, too, have shown this kind of love in their hearts. If our own times have any claim to be well thought of, it is surely because this love is strongly abroad.

It is love again when He receives the sick; when He lets that great sea of misery wash up to Him; when He lifts up, strengthens, and heals. It is love when He says, "Come to me, all you who are weary and heavily burdened, and I will give you rest."[128] Oh, this tremendous Lover and the might and majesty of His heart taking up arms against the massive world-force of sorrow, magnificently sure of His inexhaustible power to comfort, to strengthen, and to bless! Love is indeed all these things. But still we do not see the uniqueness about these several instances that bring us to say, "Love is He and He alone."

We must go deeper in our search.

That last evening before His death, those hours when what was coming hovered dark and terrible, and at the same time every happening of the past was brought sharply to the foreground of His soul's memory, Jesus was with His disciples, in a state of mind more withdrawn and interior than ever before,

---

[126] St. Francis of Assisi (c. 1182-1226), founder of the Franciscan Order.

[127] Mark 6:34.

[128] Matt. 11:28.

waiting completely on His Father's will, aware in His deepest self, of His mission and the purpose of His presence. Just before his account of that last evening, John says, "Before the paschal feast began, Jesus already knew that the time had come for His passage from this world to the Father. He still loved those who were His own, whom He was leaving in the world, and He would give them the supreme proof of His love."[129] He washed their feet; then, while they ate the Passover together, He bequeathed the mystery of His Testament.

Matthew reports it so: "And while they were still at table, Jesus took bread, and blessed and broke it, and gave it to His disciples, saying, 'Take, eat; this is my body.' Then He took a cup, and offered thanks, and gave it to them, saying, 'Drink, all of you, of this; for this is my blood, of the new testament, shed for many, to the remission of sins.' "[130] And Luke has it: "And when the time came, He sat down with His twelve disciples. And He said to them, 'I have longed to share this paschal meal with you before my Passion.' . . . Then He took bread, and blessed and broke it, and gave it to them, saying, 'This is my body, given for you; do this for a commemoration of me.' And so with the cup, when supper was ended: 'This cup,' He said, 'is the new testament, in my blood which is to be shed for you.' "[131]

Two words in these sentences must be understood at least to some extent if we are to follow what went on: the little words *for you*. The mystery that Jesus was bequeathing is imbedded

[129] John 13:1.
[130] Matt. 26:26-28.
[131] Cf. Luke 22:14-15, 17-19.

in the Passover meal, in memory of the covenant God made with His people, in those days when He sent the Angel of Destruction against Pharaoh's obduracy with the most dreadful of all plagues, the death of every firstborn. At that time, Moses was instructed that every family was to kill a lamb and paint their doorposts with its blood, and all should eat of it standing and dressed and ready for a journey. The blood was to be a sign of safety from the avenger on his way; the meal celebrated the covenant of alliance between the people and their rescuing God. That was the lamb eaten in the paschal meal of the old testament; that was the blood shed as seal of confirmation to the covenant. And now Jesus speaks of love, bestowed anew in death and a communal meal — blood shed to seal the new testament.

The victim, in the death that is to take place, is He.

"For you" — for us. These words are as if covered with ashes, gray, impotent; custom has made them so. We have heard them countless times, and their edge has gone blunt. Do we still grasp what they mean?

Any man alive stands in himself and feels himself at the natural center of things, as if the world would stop existing for him if he should cease to be. Does such a being ever give his life for another? Certainly he does. A mother does as much for her child. A man does as much for his work or his ideas. This happens now and then, one has to say; or more accurately, seldom, very seldom. More often than not, what passes as sacrifice for work or an idea is nothing but camouflaged assertion of status. Or a man may give his life for his nation, carried off by the dreadful events of war. Or he might do the same for his neighbor in peril, if he is driven by a great heart. But what about giving one's life for mankind — for all the strangers afar off, for all those he encounters who have no sympathy or understanding or love for him, who accept nothing, and who even defend themselves against the salvation being offered them?

We can have no understanding of the words *for you* until we cleanse ourselves of every trace of sentimentality. We must clarify in our minds the degree of isolation in which our Lord stood, abandoned by all who might have helped, without the stimulating atmosphere pervading great affairs, with no enthusiasm of any kind about Him, and without the support or élan of natural drives or creative compulsion. He knows that men are lost. He knows they can breathe in the freedom of salvation only when satisfaction has been made for their sins. Life may come to them only through a death which He alone can die. He takes this for granted, starts from this premise. That is what is meant by the words *for you*.

We can understand them — and it is our entire Christian duty to understand them — only if in the deepest stillness of our hearts, and the readiness of our hearts, we strive for this understanding, and God furnishes us with the necessary graces. But what Jesus achieved *for you*: that is His love.

And herein lies the mystery of the Eucharist.

When He was announcing this at Capernaum, He said, "I myself am the living bread that has come down from Heaven. If anyone eats of this bread, he shall live forever. And now, what is this bread which I am to give? It is my flesh, given for the life of the world." Then the Jews fell to disputing with one another, "How can this man give us His flesh to eat?" Whereupon Jesus said to them, "Believe me when I tell you this; you can have no life in yourselves unless you eat the flesh of the Son of Man, and drink His blood. The man who eats my flesh and drinks my blood enjoys eternal life, and I will raise him up at the last day. My flesh is real food; my blood is real drink. He who eats my flesh and drinks my blood lives continually in me and I in him. As I live because of the Father, the living Father who has sent me, so he who eats me will live, in his turn, because of me."[132]

The Gospel goes on to say that "the Jews murmured."[133] We cannot help finding this very understandable. Someone standing in their midst, very much alive, tells them in the fullness of His vigor that they must eat His flesh and drink His blood; and this audience has no confidence in Him to begin with — how could they be other than indignant and antagonistic? And when He says, "Only the spirit gives you life; the flesh is of no avail," and, "The words I have been speaking to you are spirit and life,"[134] His words can reach only those who are ready to follow along in blind confidence through the darkness.

The Eucharist is rooted in Jesus' death. It will always remain a mystery. But we can feel how we are bound to it with deeper and closer bonds by virtue of Christ's death and Resurrection. He even said so Himself: "Does this try your faith? What will you make of it if you see the Son of Man ascending to the place where He was before?[135] By His death and Resurrection, Jesus

---

[132] John 6:51-58 (RSV = John 6:51-57).

[133] John 6:41.

[134] John 6:64 (RSV = John 6:63).

[135] John 6:62-63 (RSV = John 6:61-62).

underwent a transfiguration, into His spiritual mode of being. He lives as one glorified in the Eucharist. The Eucharist proceeds from His death. Not for nothing does St. Paul write in his first letter to the Corinthians: "It is the Lord's death that you are heralding, whenever you eat this bread and drink this cup, until He comes."[136]

The gift of the Eucharist and our Lord's death are, in the deepest sense, one and the same mystery. The love that drove Him to die for us was the same love that made Him give us Himself as nourishment. It was not enough to give us gifts, words, and instructions; He gave us Himself as well.

Perhaps we must seek out woman, the loving mother, to find someone who understands this kind of longing: to give not some *thing*, but rather oneself — to give oneself, with all one's being; not only the spirit, not only one's fidelity, but body and soul, flesh and blood, everything. This is indeed the ultimate love: to want to feed others with the very substance of one's own self. And for that, our Lord went to His death, so that He might rise again in the Resurrection, in that condition wherein He desired to give Himself to all mankind for evermore.

And now He who died for us lives again, within us. In His farewell we read, "I am the true vine, and it is my Father who tends it. The branch that yields no fruit in me He cuts away; the branch that does yield fruit He trims clean, so that it may yield more fruit. You, through the message I have preached to you, are clean already; you have only to live on in me, and I will live on in you. The branch that does not live on in the vine can yield no fruit of itself; no more can you, if you do not

---

[136] 1 Cor. 11:26.

live on in me. I am the vine; you are its branches. If a man lives on in me, and I in him, he will yield abundant fruit; separated from me, you have no power to do anything."[137]

He has gone into us, and works within us, and we live in Him and by Him, just as the vine's branch bears the leaf and fruit from out of the living interdependency of its entire growth.

St. Paul placed this mystery at the foundation of all Christian being. He says, "You know well enough that we who were taken up into Christ by Baptism have been taken up, all of us, into His death. In our Baptism, we have been buried with Him, died like Him, so, just as Christ was raised up from the dead by His Father's power, we, too, might live and move in a new kind of existence. We have to be closely fitted into the pattern of His Resurrection, as we have been into the pattern of His death; we have to be sure of this, that our former nature has been crucified with Him, and the living power of our guilt annihilated, so that we are the slaves of guilt no longer. Guilt makes no more claim on a man who is dead. And if we have died with Christ, we have faith to believe that we shall share His life.

"We know that Christ, now that He has risen from the dead, cannot die anymore; death has no more power over Him; the death He died was a death, once for all, to sin; the life He now lives is a life that looks toward God. And you, too, must think of yourselves as dead to sin, and alive with a life that looks toward God, through Christ Jesus our Lord."[138]

[137] John 15:1-5.
[138] Rom. 6:3-11.

"And yet I am alive! Or rather, not I; it is Christ who lives in me."[139] The whole life of Christ recapitulates itself ever anew in man. To live as a Christian means to participate in the re-enactment of Christ's life. This happens every time a believer takes a step closer to the Lord, whenever he conquers himself in the course of following Christ. When he carries out within himself the Lord's commandment, something dies within him: the old man. And something rises up: the new man, "made after the fashion of Christ." Christ rises within him. And so on, ever the same. Until such time as there slowly grows up within him "the glory of a child of God," "made after the image and likeness of Christ,"[140] at first invisible, concealed, covered over with ashes and debris, frustrated, imperiled; but then gradually growing stronger until finally it is revealed, after this death, and the old man drops away forever.

That is Christ's love: that He lives in us in this way, and we in Him, and what is His and what is ours becomes one. That is what Christ's love is: the love of the Redeemer who dies for us; the love which bestows itself, which gives its all, body and soul, for us to feed upon; the love of being within us, so that His life becomes our life, and ours His.

That is what Christ's love is. And it is only in the light that shines hence that all else that had to do with love in His life takes on clarity in the plan or design of Christ's love: how He called to Himself the weary and oppressed that He might comfort them; how He took unto Himself all the sufferings of mankind, bringing relief; how He cast His mercy over the dark

[139] Gal. 2:20.
[140] Cf. Rom. 8:21, 29.

distress of nations; how He showed tenderness for all living things, plants, and animals: the first kind of love we spoke of shows in all these instances. That is the love that is revealed in them.

Chapter Twelve

Recognizing the Presence of Jesus in Every Moment

Blessed are those
who have not seen, and
yet have learned to believe.
John 20:29

∞

A very beautiful portion of St. John's Gospel takes us to the midst of that mystery-charged time between the Lord's Resurrection and His quitting the world. At that moment, the disciples must have felt they were both in and out of this central fact of history; they must have had to ask themselves over and over again whether or not what they saw before their eyes was really and truly happening; and yet these events were impressing themselves upon them more intensely than reality. It was a time when their innermost being was disengaging from the associations and obligations of the dying world of the Old Testament, and turning toward a new order of things whose direction they could not yet understand.

It was a strange life they led — frightened and at the same time full of boundless hope. Soon they were to be in the room together, soon by the sea; soon they would be walking on the streets — and time and again, they would encounter this mysterious Figure, suddenly, as if out of another world. The Figure speaks to them, instructs them, plays upon them with the exhalation of His power.

So at one point they were seated in a room together, the doors bolted for fear of the Jews. It was still only a few days since the Lord had been put to death. Unrest was abroad. It had in fact received a fresh impetus from the strange news that had come from the grave. And there Jesus stood in the room right in their midst, and wished them peace.

"Peace be upon you."[141] These words make us reflect. Jesus had indeed said the very opposite: "I come not to bring peace, but a sword."[142] And both are true. Whoever comes to Jesus receives His peace — "that peace that the world cannot give";[143] the peace that consists of the believer's certainty that God exists, God lives. God is He Himself, the one and only; and He loves me, and nothing can tear me from His love. But the sword is also there. The coming of Christ, the summons from God, does not permit the one who is called to go on living as he pleases. He has a rude awakening from his peaceful earthly existence, disrupts his ways, and turns away from many things that are charming and beautiful in themselves. Peace and a sword: Christ brings both. Both are names for the one thing whereby God comes to us in Him, draws us to Him.

The disciples were frightened; they did not know whether it was He or, as it says in another passage, a ghost.[144] His presence produced shock. His presence filled them with fear. What could it be, that went through one so? Is it He or something else? He calmed them down. He showed them His hands and His side. They recognized Him and were glad.

Once again He bade them be at peace. This time He meant peace toward the world outside as well. They were to carry His message out into the world, as well as that sword which always

---

[141] John 20:21.
[142] Matt. 10:34.
[143] Cf. John 14:27.
[144] Luke 24:37.

goes together with the peace of Christ. "I came upon an errand from my Father, and now I am sending you out in my turn." They were not to carry out the Word alone, but the living power of God itself, the very peace, the very sword: "With that He breathed on them and said to them, 'Receive the Holy Spirit.' " He bestowed on them the effective principle that worked within Him, the power of God's Spirit, which touches the very heart, releases, and fulfills — the power that purifies and heals: "When you forgive men's sins, they are forgiven."[145]

"There was one of the twelve, Thomas, who is also called Didymus, who was not with them when Jesus came. And when the other disciples told him, 'We have seen the Lord,' he said to them, 'Until I have seen the marks of the nails on His hands, until I have put my finger into the mark of the nails, and put my hand into His side, you will never make me believe.' "[146] Thomas appears to have been a realist: reserved, cool, and perhaps a little obstinate.

The days went by, and the disciples went on living under this considerable tension. After a week, they were together again in the house, and this time Thomas was with them. The same thing repeated itself. Jesus passed through closed doors, stepped into their midst, and spoke: "Peace be upon you." Then He called the man who was struggling against faith: "Let me have thy finger; see, here are my hands. Let me have thy hand; put it into my side. Cease thy doubting, and believe!" At this point, Thomas was overwhelmed. The truth of it all came home to him: this man standing before him, so moving,

---

[145] John 20:20-23.
[146] John 20:24-25.

arousing such deep feelings within him, this man so full of mystery, so different from all other men — He is the very same one they used to be together with, who was put to death a short time ago. And Thomas surrendered: "Thou art my Lord and my God!" Thomas believed.

Then we come upon the strange words: "And Jesus said to him, "Thou hast learned to believe, Thomas, because thou hast seen me. Blessed are those who have not seen, and yet have learned to believe.' "[147]

Such words as these are really extraordinary! Thomas believed because he saw. But our Lord did not call him blessed. He had been allowed to see — to see the hands and the side, and to touch the blessed wounds, yet he was not blessed!

Perhaps Thomas had a narrow escape from a great danger. He wanted proofs, wanted to see and touch; but then, too, it might have been rebellion deep within him, the vainglory of an intelligence that would not surrender, a sluggishness and coldness of heart. He got what he asked for: a look and a touch. But it must have been a concession he deplored having received, when he thought on it afterward. He could have believed and been saved, not because he got what he demanded; he could have believed because God's mercy had touched his heart and given him the grace of interior vision, the gift of the opening of the heart, and of its surrender.

God could also have let him stay with the words he had spoken: in that state of unbelief which cuts itself off from everything, that insists on human evidence to become convinced. In that case, he would have remained an unbeliever

[147] John 20:26-29.

and gone on his way. In that state, external seeing and touch-ing would not have helped him at all; he simply would have called it delusion. Nothing that comes from God, even the greatest miracle, proves out like two times two. It touches a person; it is only seen and grasped when the heart is open and the spirit is purged of self. Then it awakens faith. But when these conditions are not present, there are always reasons to be found to say solemnly and impressively that it is all delusion, or that such-and-such is so because some other thing is so. Or, the excuse that is always handy: We cannot explain it yet; the future will enlighten us about it.

Thomas was standing a hair's breadth away from obduracy and perdition. He was not at all blessed.

Blessed indeed are "those who have not seen, and yet have learned to believe." Those who ask for no miracles, demand nothing out of the ordinary, but who find God's message in everyday life. Those who require no compelling proofs, but who know that everything coming from God must remain in a certain ultimate suspense, so that faith may never cease to re-quire daring. Those who know that the heart is not overcome by faith, that there is no force or violence there, compelling belief by rigid certitudes. What comes from God touches gently, comes quietly, does not disturb freedom, and leads to quiet, profound, peaceful resolve within the heart. And those are called blessed who make the effort to remain open-hearted; who seek to cleanse their hearts of all self-righteousness, obsti-nacy, presumption, and inclination to "know better"; who are quick to hear, humble, and free-spirited. Those are called blessed who are able to find God's message in the Gospel for the day, or even from the sermons of preachers with no message in particular; or in phrases from the Law they have heard a thousand times, phrases with no quality of charismatic power about them; or in the happenings of everyday life which always end up the same way: work and rest, anxiety — and then again some kind of success, some joy, an encounter, and a sorrow.

Blessed are those who can see the Lord in all these things!

Chapter Thirteen

∾

How Jesus Makes Heaven Present to Us Today

Now I am leaving
the world and going
on my way to the Father.
John 16:28

∞

The Lord died and arose from the dead to a new life of an absolutely Godlike character. It was that life that was suddenly and mysteriously illuminated for a moment on Mount Tabor.[148] When He was on His way to Jerusalem, where He was to suffer, this Godlike essence blazed up from hidden depths. True enough, it was only for one short hour, and thereafter it subsided. Now, however, after He had walked through death, life broke through with almighty power. The Lord lived. Now He lived in a new way — alive from within, with a divine Lordship permeating His being, body and soul.

Now there was a strange interval of time. He was still on earth, and yet no longer so. He had a way of appearing, first in one place, then in another; making mysterious transitions from some otherwhere into the here, and then disappearing again. He had overcome the limitations of earthly existence. Gravity no longer bound Him. Space and the resistant quality of material substance could not interfere with Him. Yet He still lived on earth.

Finally He took definite leave of earth, for Heaven.

What is Heaven? When one asks a child that question, the child will just point upward: "Up there." We should not be too

---

[148] Matt. 17:2; Mark 9:2.

swift to laugh. The child means more by those words than may be established by the metamorphosis of scientific investigation; that "up there" which cannot exist because there is no such thing as up and down in the last analysis — if the child were questioned more exactingly, the answer would be: "Heaven is where God lives."

Could we have any better answer, any truer one, to the question of what Heaven is than this one: that Heaven is where God lives? When our Lord spoke of His forthcoming death, did He not say, "I leave the world and go to the Father"?

But if Heaven is where God lives, and God is everywhere, then it must follow that Heaven is everywhere. That is quite true. Heaven is everywhere. In every place, and here, too. That is the first and greatest answer: Heaven is right here.

Again, this was said by Jesus Himself: "The kingdom of Heaven is within you."[149] How is this so? God is supposed to live in the "inaccessible light."[150] That is true. By ourselves, we cannot get in. It is closed. Heaven is all about us, yet it is closed to us.

It was open around Jesus. He entered into this openness when He left us; and then He was gone.

Heaven is where God lives. Heaven is the presence of God. Now He has opened this presence to us.

Can there be a presence which is closed? Yes, there is such a thing. When I want to approach someone, I can always travel to the town where he lives and go to his house; I can sit down beside him. Then I am together with him. But if his attention

[149] Luke 17:21.
[150] 1 Tim. 6:16.

is elsewhere, or if he has no confidence in me, then despite all physical proximity in space, he is in fact so far away that I cannot possibly "get to him." That is presence closed off.

It would open up, as it were, if he took notice of me, felt some sympathy, trust, or affection for me; then this presence would be an open thing, and he alone can create this condition of accessible proximity. It can come only from him, yet it is part of the picture that I should feel it too. I must notice how he directs his attention toward me; I must respond to his affection and trust. Then, when one has become inwardly involved with the other, has developed a sympathetic response to the other's thoughts and emotions, there is true proximity.

God is always and everywhere near to man. But to man by himself, His presence is inaccessible, blocked off. God alone can open up this channel. We believe He did this. The presence of the Father was all around Jesus. The Father was completely open with Him, one with Him in an infinity of love. We have listened to the words whence this presence can be heard speaking out. Heaven surrounded Jesus, the accessible presence of the Father.

And Jesus has brought this presence to us. We know that the Father loves us in Jesus. We have confidence in the grace of His love for us; we know that His eyes see us, His heart is turned toward us, and His hand leads us. We believe that Heaven is around us.

However, one thing is missing: we do not *feel* the presence of God. It is still closed off, from our side. It is closed off by what we ourselves are; by the heaviness of our imprisoned being; by the slothfulness and dullness of our hearts; by the evil that is in us. Heaven would be here entire if God opened up

His presence to us, and at the same time opened up men's hearts so they could feel this presence.

Perhaps it can be said that Heaven is on its way to us as long as we do not keep it at a distance by our own actions. I believe it is no fantasy or delusion to think this way: that our whole Christian life consists in having Heaven continually striving to catch up with us, close in on us. Every Christian act, belief, love, sacrifice, struggle, every perseverance and courageous performance — all these things make possible the approach of Him who desires only to come forward. But all coldness, indifference, slothfulness, weakness, pride, covetousness — everything that sin is called — forces Him back, bars the road to Him. And Heaven fights. Heaven wants to come to us. For Heaven is only God's love come home.

What a tremendous thought it is: Heaven on the way to meet me, relentlessly advancing toward me, and God's eye is upon me. And to think of the mightiness of the will behind it! The monumental strength of that desire! From what depths comes that petition: "Thy kingdom come"[151] — the kingdom of Heaven!

When is Heaven truly and completely present? It is when all heaviness is gone; when all sluggishness has been overcome, all wickedness, coldness, pride, irritation, disobedience, and covetousness; when there is no danger anymore of falling away; when grace has made one's whole being open up, body and soul, to the ultimate profundities; when there is no further danger that it will all close in again, become hardened in ways of evil; when all work to be done on earth is finished, and all

[151] Matt. 6:10; Luke 11:2.

guilt has been paid by repentance. What all this means is: after death.

After death — when time is no longer; when everything is in the everlasting now; when nothing can change anymore, but the creature stands illuminated by the light of eternity, before God — at that time, everything will be open, and will remain so. That is being in Heaven.

The day He left this earth, Jesus went to Heaven, His body and His soul. All earthly heaviness vanished. All limitations of being in this place or that place dropped away. Every burden of earthly need fell away. There was nothing more closed off, not even for the body. Everything was open. Everything about Him made its way in the overmastering presence of His Father.

But here is the mystery: the very moment that He leaves us, He returns: "I am going away" to the Father; but He added immediately "and coming back to you."[152] And in Matthew's Gospel, He told them, "Behold I am with you all the days that are coming, till the consummation of the world."[153] And the one statement is made true by the other. He went away from us, His body also, to Heaven, to the pure and open presence of His Father which He has directed toward us. He who was the intermediary between the Father and us — "the way, the truth and the life"[154] — has entered completely into this love. Now He is everywhere the Father's love is, and so He is with us. He is gone from the visible, transient here and now. But now, from there, and because He is there, He can, through the love of the

[152] John 14:28.
[153] Matt. 28:20.
[154] John 14:6.

The Inner Life of Jesus

Father, be with each of us and with the Father also. He is within us, closing in upon us, bringing with Him the presence of the Father, Heaven.

"See where I stand at the door, knocking; if anyone listens to my voice and opens the door, I will come in to visit him, and make my supper with him, and he shall sup with me."[155] "Supper" is the extravagant superabundance of God's accessible presence bursting in, blessed, satisfying, making drunk with all the drunkenness of love.

This is how we properly understand Heaven. It is that close presence wherein the Father stands in relation to Jesus Christ. And Heaven for us will be participation in this intimacy of love. This condition is already beginning; it approaches closer; now in peril, it is fought over, lost, and won back again. So it goes with our Christian life.

[155]Rev. 3:20.

∞

Biographical Note

Romano Guardini
(1885-1968)

Although he was born in Verona, Italy, Romano Guardini grew up in Mainz, Germany, where his father was serving as Italian consul. Since his education and formation were German, he decided to remain in Germany as an adult.

After studying chemistry and economics in his youth, Guardini turned to theology and was ordained to the priesthood in 1910. From 1923 to 1939 (when he was expelled by the Nazis), Father Guardini occupied a chair especially created for him at the University of Berlin as "professor for philosophy of religion and Catholic *Weltanschauung*." After the war, similar positions were created for him — first at the University of Tübingen and then at the University of Munich (1948-1963).

Father Guardini's extremely popular courses in these universities won him a reputation as one of the most remarkable and successful Catholic educators in Germany. As a teacher, writer, and speaker, he was notable for being able to detect and nurture those elements of spirituality that nourish all that is best in the life of Catholics. After the war, Father Guardini's influence grew to be enormous, not only through his university positions, but also through the inspiration and guidance he gave to the postwar German Catholic Youth Movement, which enlivened the faith of countless young people.

The Inner Life of Jesus

Father Guardini's writings include works on meditation, education, literature, art, philosophy, and theology. Among his dozens of books, perhaps the most famous is *The Lord*, which has been continuously in print in many languages since its first publication in 1937.

Even today, countless readers continue to be transformed by these books, which combine a profound thirst for God with great depth of thought and a delightful perfection of expression. The works of Father Guardini are indispensable reading for anyone who wants to remain true to the Faith and to grow holy in our age of skepticism and corrosive doubt.

∞

Sophia Institute Press®